Encyclopedia of
Bible Truths

Ruth C. Haycock

[Fine Arts/Health]

Books, Textbooks, and Educational Resources for Christian Educators and Schools Worldwide

© 1993 by Association of Christian Schools International/Purposeful Design Publications
Reprinted 2005
Printed in the United States of America
10 09 08 07 06 05   1 2 3 4 5 6 7

Unless otherwise noted, all Scripture quotations are from *The Holy Bible, New King James Version* (NKJV), © 1982 by Thomas Nelson, Inc., used by permission, all rights reserved; and *The Holy Bible, King James Version*. Other versions include the *New American Standard Bible* (NASB), © 1960, 1962, 1963, 1968, 1971, 1972, 1973, 1975, 1977 by The Lockman Foundation.

Purposeful Design Publications is the publishing division of ACSI and is committed to the ministry of Christian school education, to enable Christian educators and schools worldwide to effectively prepare students for life. As the publisher of books, textbooks, and other educational resources within ACSI, Purposeful Design Publications strives to produce biblically sound materials that reflect Christian scholarship and stewardship and that address the identified needs of Christian schools around the world.

Encyclopedia of Bible Truths—Fine Arts/Health

ISBN 1-58331-137-8   Catalog #6520-D

Purposeful Design Publications
A Division of ACSI
PO Box 65130 • Colorado Springs, CO 80962-5130
www.acsi.org

Foreword

Christian schooling today is impacting the lives of countless numbers of students around the world. It is focused upon developing a Christian worldview through the careful and articulate integration of God's Word into the broader academic curriculum. Christ-centered schools are effectively changing young lives for the cause of Christ. Regardless of the subject being taught, when permeated with scriptural principles, a worldview is being intricately etched in the students' hearts and minds, impacting their thinking and decision making for a lifetime. This book has been carefully designed to assist you in helping make that crucial connection between each of the academic disciplines and God's Word.

The *Encyclopedia of Bible Truths* is the work of Dr. Ruth Haycock, a gifted researcher, writer, and Christian teacher. She devoted her entire adult life to the compilation of the valuable information contained in these pages. Ruth Haycock is now in heaven, enjoying the eternal rewards of her selfless and sacrificial service, while Christian educators worldwide have the opportunity to strengthen their own teaching with the support of this book.

It has never been intended that the *Encyclopedia of Bible Truths* be the sole resource for biblical integration in the Christian school classroom, but this resource has been designed to provide that needed assistance in most subject areas for lesson preparation and project assignments. As you use this valuable resource, it is our desire that the relevance and truth of God's Word will come alive as students experience the empowered teaching of biblically integrated academic courses.

It is a privilege to commend this powerful teaching resource as you prepare your students *for such a time as this.*

Ken Smitherman, LLD
President
Association of Christian Schools International

Introduction

It has often been said, *"The Christian student attending a secular school is being sheltered from the truth; consequently he is conforming to the world rather than to the image of Christ."* In a general way, those of us involved in Christian schools are quick to agree, recognizing that without the written Word, the Bible, and the living Word, Jesus Christ, a child is being cheated. He is not getting the things in life which are most crucial to his becoming what God intends.

Even in a Christian school, however, it is possible that a child may be sheltered from truth, especially in his academic studies. He may be involved in Bible class and chapel, be subject to Christian standards and discipline, be active in Christian service, and still be getting primarily a secular academic education. What he is taught, and how he is taught, may be so similar to what is done in the neighboring non-Christian school that a visitor would not detect a difference.

As Christian schools have multiplied, many Bible-believing teachers have moved from public schools to Christian schools. They have rejoiced in the freedom to mention the Lord and all that is most precious to them. They have been happy for higher standards of discipline and achievement. In many cases, though, they have brought to their new schools the same old perspectives on their subjects. It is, in many cases, the only thing they know. They learned it in the public schools themselves. They built upon that foundation in college. They learned how to teach it and then for some years used the secular humanist textbooks and teacher's manuals which were provided.

New teachers, too, have often had all their training either in secular institutions or in Christian colleges where their education professors were the products of humanistic colleges and graduate schools. Too frequently a typical thought is, *"After all, social studies is social studies, isn't it, regardless of where you teach it, so why expect a different social studies in a Christian school?"* Of course, this same attitude is expressed about nearly every other curricular area.

If we actually believe that the Bible is authoritative in every subject it addresses, in history and science as well as in Christian doctrine, we are obligated to find out what it says about every topic we teach. If we fail to present what God says but teach other aspects of a subject, we shelter pupils from the truth and give them only part of the story.

What we do teach may be purely humanistic and opposed to the truth found in the Bible, or it may be true as far as it goes, but incomplete. In either case, students' thinking is being shaped according to the world's pattern. God asks instead for transformed lives, not conformed to the world but based on renewed minds able to prove what is that good and acceptable and perfect will of God.

If Christian schools are to be Christian in the academic areas and to present a biblical life and worldview, teachers must become increasingly familiar with what the Word says on each subject; they need to search for ways to involve students in learning, ways which enable them to understand and accept that biblical viewpoint that is part of God's perfect will. In addition, Christian teachers must assist one another in producing textbooks and other materials based on biblical principles.

It is not enough that we moralize in Bible classes to teach socially acceptable or even Christian conduct. Neither is it adequate that we use incidents from history, or observations from science, to illustrate spiritual truth. Though history and science furnish many possible object lessons, their use in this fashion is not a true integration of truth from Scripture and truth from other sources. It is not equivalent to searching out what God actually teaches about money, or capital punishment, or the treatment of animals, and then teaching it as part of the academic study of that topic.

Again, neither does the use of sentences from the Bible in a grammar lesson, or scriptural words in a spelling lesson, necessarily mean that a biblical view is taught. The frequent quotation of Bible verses in workbooks or textbooks, or the use of biblical themes from artwork, does not guarantee that the subject itself is being taught biblically. While education in a Christian school should surely include a study of Bible sentences and words and the use of biblical quotations and themes, the integration of truth is a much deeper matter.

Basic to the whole concept of teaching God's truth in every area, and of helping students to see all truth as from God, are two prerequisites for the Christian school. First, the Bible must be thoroughly taught at each grade level as the inerrant Word of God, whether it deals with evangelism or economics. Second, Christian aspects of a subject must be included as part of that academic discipline, not relegated to Bible class alone.

For example, as the literary classics are studied, Christian writings must be included; as the Middle East is considered historically or geographically, Palestine and Israel must be given a rightful place. To fail here is to say to young people that the Bible and academic subjects are separate—that only in Bible class do we consider what God says. With such a message conveyed to them, students will graduate with what some have called intellectual schizophrenia, and defeat the whole purpose of the Christian school.

The compilation of principles and supporting Scripture passages included in this book on a subject-by-subject basis are intended to stimulate the study of each subject in the Word of God as well as in other sources. May He guide your steps and give you understanding.

Ruth C. Haycock

Contents

Foreword by ACSI President Ken Smitherman, LLD

Introduction by Dr. Ruth C. Haycock

Fine Arts/Health

Creativity

[Fine Arts/Health]

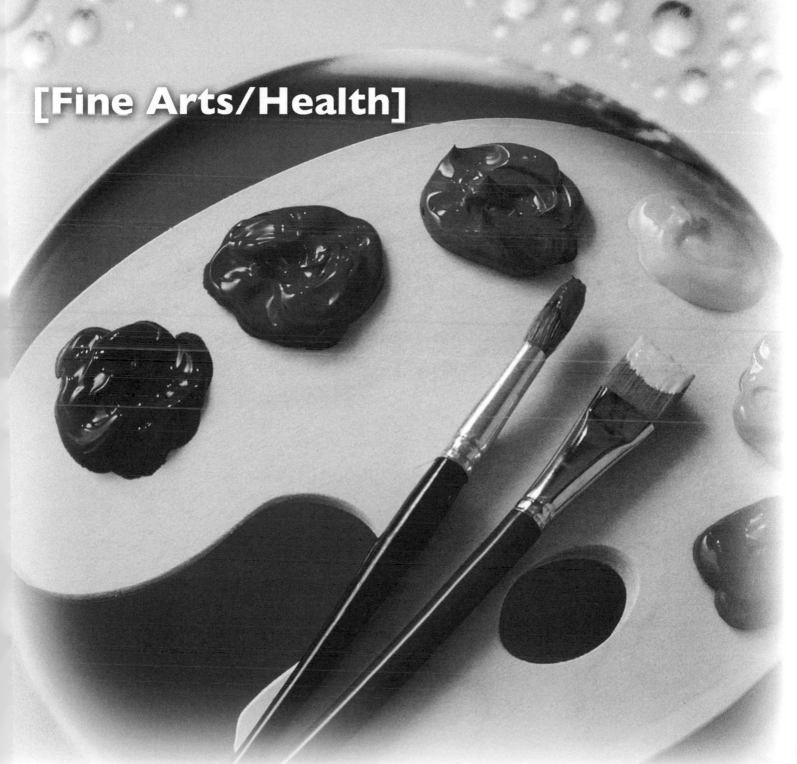

Creativity: Biblical Concepts

I. GOD'S CREATIVITY

1. Creation is God's artwork; He was the first creator.
2. God evaluated His creative works when they were finished.
3. God's creations communicate His truth and love to man.
4. God's creations offer both enjoyment and instruction.
5. God created man with the ability to produce and appreciate beauty.
6. God gives a variety of specialized abilities which are creative in nature.
7. God underscores the importance of creativity when He gives us the record of the human originators.

II. MAN'S CREATIVITY

1. Man's creations are the expressions of his inner thoughts and feelings.
2. Man's creativity is more limited than God's.
   a. It is limited to working with what God has already created.
   b. It is limited to creating things, things which do not themselves have the capacity to create.
3. Creativity involves the power of choice; it is an indication of freedom, at least within limits.
4. Man's varied creative abilities demonstrate the uniqueness of each person.
5. Man's creativity and his ability to appreciate the creativity of others are affected by sin.

III. OUR RESPONSIBILITY

1. We should draw closer to God and understand Him better through study of His creation.
2. We are responsible to think on beautiful things and to appreciate the beauty God has provided.
   a. God gives a specific command; we are to respond differently from the world.
   b. God calls to our attention some aspects of His creation that we should think about.
3. We must discern between what pleases God and what does not glorify Him; we must ask, "Does this reflect God and His beauty?"
   a. God directs that we should specifically seek those things which glorify Him.
   b. God also warns us against those things which pollute our minds and hearts, drawing us away from Him.
4. We should yield our abilities to God to be used for His glory, whether in enjoyment and appreciation, or in production of that for which He has given us the ability.
   a. Statements and examples which apply to every believer.
   b. Statements concerning yieldedness of special abilities to Him, not the same for all believers.
5. We must recognize God's evaluation of physical beauty, whether of the human body or of things, in contrast with spiritual beauty, or the beauty of character.
   a. The danger of too much emphasis on physical beauty.
   b. The importance of spiritual beauty, the beauty of a holy life.

> *"No work of art is more important than the Christian's own life, and every Christian is called upon to be an artist in this sense. He may have no gift of creativity in terms of the way he lives his life. In this sense, the Christian life is to be a thing of truth and also a thing of beauty in the midst of a lost and despairing world."*
> —Francis A. Schaeffer, *Art and the Bible,* p. 63.

Creativity: Biblical Background

I. GOD'S CREATIVITY

1. Creation is God's artwork; He was the first creator.

Genesis 1–2

Here we have the account of God's creation of the heavens and the earth, the dry land, plant life, sun, moon, stars, animal life, man and woman.

Genesis 2:8–9

8The LORD God planted a garden eastward in Eden.... 9And out of the ground the LORD God made every tree grow that is pleasant to the sight and good for food....

Psalm 135:6

Whatever the LORD pleases He does, In heaven and in earth, In the seas and in all deep places.

Psalm 139:14

I will praise You; for I am fearfully and wonderfully made: Marvelous are Your works; and that my soul knows very well.

John 1:3

All things were made through Him; and without Him nothing was made that was made.

Colossians 1:16–17

16For by Him all things were created that are in heaven and that are on earth, visible and invisible, whether thrones or dominions or principalities or powers. All things were created through Him and for Him: 17And he is before all things, and in Him all things consist [or hold together].

(For further references to God's creative work, see Volume III of this series, on Science and Mathematics.)

2. God evaluated His creative works when they were finished.

Genesis 1:4, 10, 12, 18, 21, 25, 31

4And God saw the light, that it was good... 10And God called the dry land Earth, and the gathering together of the waters He called Seas. And God saw that it was good.... 12And the earth brought forth grass, the herb...and the tree that yields fruit...And God saw that it was good.... 16Then God made two great lights...He made the stars also. 18...And God saw that it was good.... 21So God created great sea creatures and every living thing that moves, with which the waters abounded, according to their kind, and every winged bird according to its kind. And God saw that it was good.... 25And God made the beast...cattle...and every thing that creeps...And God saw that it was good.... 31Then God saw everything that He had made, and, indeed, it was very good.

3. God's creations communicate His truth and love to man.

Exodus 31:18, 32:15–16

18He gave Moses two tablets of the Testimony, tables of stone, written with the finger of God. 15And Moses turned, and went down from the mountain, and the two tablets of the Testimony were in his hand. The tables were written on both sides; on the one side and on the other were they written. 16Now the tablets were the work of God, and the writing was the writing of God engraved on the tablets.

Psalm 19:1–3

1The heavens declare the glory of God; and the firmament shows His handiwork. 2Day unto day utters speech, and night unto night reveals knowledge. 3There is no speech nor language, where their voice is not heard.

Psalm 145:10

All Your works shall praise You, O LORD.

Psalm 148:5

Let them [i.e., the heavenly bodies, the angels, the waters above the heavens] praise the name of the LORD: for He commanded, and they were created.

Isaiah 40:26

Lift up your eyes on high, and see who has

created these things, Who brings out their host by number; He call them all by name, by the greatness of His might and the strength of His power; not one is missing.

Romans 1:20

For since the creation of the world His invisible attributes are clearly seen, being understood by the things that are made, even His eternal power and Godhead, so that they are without excuse.

(See also Edith Schaeffer's *Hidden Art,* chapter 1, "The First Artist.")

4. God's creations offer both enjoyment and instruction.

Genesis 15:5

God uses the stars of the sky, which Abraham had doubtless marveled at many times, to demonstrate His promise of descendants: *⁵Then He brought him outside and said, "Look now toward heaven, and count the stars if you are able to number them." And He said to him, "So shall your descendants be."*

Genesis 32:12

Two generations later, God renewed his promise to Jacob with these words: *¹²I will surely treat you well, and make your descendants as the sand of the sea, which cannot be numbered for multitude.*

Job 12:7–10

Job, in answering the arguments of his friends, calls attention to beasts, birds, fish, and the earth itself—all God's creations—as a source of information and understanding.

Psalm 8:3–4; 19:1–6

David's testimony: *³When I consider Your heavens, the work of Your fingers, The moon and the stars, which You have ordained: ⁴What is man, that You are mindful of him?... ¹⁹:¹The heavens declare the glory of God, and the firmament shows His handiwork.*

Proverbs 6:6–8; 30:24–28

God calls attention to the ant, the cony or badger, the locust and the spider [translated lizard in NASB], *His creations, each with specific characteristics worthy of consideration.*

See also Matthew 6:26–30; Romans 1:20.

5. God created man with the ability to produce and appreciate beauty.

Genesis 1:27

So God created man in His own image, in the image of God He created him.... Therefore man, too, was creative from the beginning.

Genesis 2:9

And out of the ground the LORD God made every tree grow that is pleasant to the sight... Only if man had a capacity for appreciation could trees be pleasant to the sight.

Genesis 4:21–22

²¹... [Jubal] was the father of all those who play the harp and flute. ²²...Tubal–cain, an instructer of every craftsman in bronze and iron... This was very early in the history of man.

Exodus 25–28

The detailed description of the tabernacle and the instructions for its construction indicate that God knew that man had the ability to do what He asked in many areas of creativity.

Exodus 25:8–9

⁸And let them make Me a sanctuary; that I may dwell among them. ⁹According to all that I show you, that is, the pattern of the tabernacle, and the pattern of all its furnishings, just so you shall make it.

6. God gives a variety of specialized abilities which are creative in nature.

a. In specific instances the source of an ability is stated as coming from God.

Examples:

Exodus 28:3

So you shall speak to all who are gifted artisans, whom I have filled with the spirit of wisdom, that they may make Aaron's garments, to sanctify him, that he may minister to Me as priest.

Exodus 31:1–6 (See also 35:30–35.)

¹And the LORD spoke to Moses, saying, ²"See, I have called by name Bezaleel... ³And I have filled him with the spirit of God, in wisdom, in understanding, in knowledge, and in all manner of workmanship, ⁴To design artistic works, to work in gold, in silver, in bronze, ⁵In cutting jewels for setting, in carving wood, and to work in all manner of workmanship ⁶indeed I, have appointed with him Aholiab...and I have put wisdom in the hearts of all who are gifted artisans, that they may make all that I have commanded you." [Then follows a list in verses 7-11.]

Exodus 36:1–2

¹And Bezaleel and Aholiab, and every gifted artisan in whom the LORD has put wisdom and understanding, to know how to do all manner of work for the service of the sanctuary, shall do according to all that the LORD has commanded. ²Then Moses called Bezaleel and Aholiab, and every gifted artisan in whose heart the LORD had put wisdom, everyone whose heart was stirred, to come and do the work. [In chapters 36–39 is the description of all that they did.]

1 Kings 4:29–34

²⁹And God gave Solomon wisdom and exceedingly great understanding, and largeness of heart like the sand on the seashore. ³⁰Thus Solomon's wisdom excelled the wisdom of all the men of the East and all the wisdom of Egypt. ³¹For he was wiser than all men... ³²He spoke three thousand proverbs, and his songs were one thousand and five...[Solomon's wisdom gift from God included ability to write poems and proverbs, as well as to judge his people.]

b. In addition, many abilities of specific kinds are mentioned in Scripture, though without any specific statement of God's special gift.

Some of these are listed in later sections dealing with art and music.

> *"What is actually made in a given society is the key to the governing conception of the purpose of life in that society...."*
> —Amanda Coomaraswamy, *Christian and Oriental Philosophy of Art* (N.Y.: Dover Publications), p. 25.

> *"God's creative activity went far beyond the minimum requirements for getting the job done. Butterflies in the rain forest seldom seen by human eyes are creatures of breathtaking beauty. The delicate transparency of the man-of-war and the hummingbird's wing are inimitable..."*
> —LeRoy Koopman, source unknown.

7. **God underscores the importance of creativity when He gives us the record of the human originators.**

Genesis 4:21–22 (quoted previously)

The following relationship may be of interest:

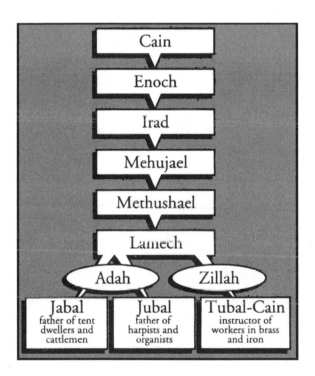

II. MAN'S CREATIVITY

1. **Man's creations are the expressions of his inner thoughts and feelings.**

Proverbs 4:23

Keep your heart with all diligence; for out of it spring the issues of life.

Matthew 12:33–35

³³Either make the tree good, and its fruit good; or else make the tree bad, and his fruit bad: for a tree is known by its fruit. ³⁴...out of the abundance of the heart the mouth speaks. ³⁵A good man out of the good treasure of his heart brings forth good things, and an evil man out of the evil treasure brings forth evil things. [While the primary emphasis here is on our speech being a portrayal of our inward being, the principle logically applies also to other expressions.]

Matthew 15:19

For out of the heart proceed evil thoughts, murders, adulteries, fornications, thefts, false witness, blasphemies. (See also Mark 7:20–23.)

Matthew 23:25–28

²⁶Blind Pharisee, first cleanse the inside of the cup and dish, that the outside of them may be clean also.

See also Chapter 3, III, Concept 5.

---

2. Man's creativity is more limited than God's.

---

a. It is limited to working with what God has already created.

Genesis 3:7

Man's first recorded creations were aprons made of fig leaves, fig leaves created by God.

Genesis 2:8–9

Only God could plant that first garden and make every tree to grow there—trees for pleasure and for food. With these man worked.

Genesis 2:18–23

Only God could make Eve as one who was of the same nature as Adam, and could therefore have fellowship with him.

Job 38:1, 4–7, 19–23, 28–32, 39:13, 26–27, 40:15–19

God mentions a variety of things that He made that were beyond Job's ability to make: the foundations of the earth, light and darkness, snow and hail, rain, ice, frost, constellations, birds, horses.

Job 42:2

Job acknowledges God's superior ability: *I know that You can do everything, and that no purpose of Yours can be withheld from You.*

b. It is limited to creating things, things which do not themselves have the capacity to create.

---

3. Creativity involves the power of choice; it is an indication of freedom, at least within limits.

Examples:

Genesis 1:3, 6, 9, 11, 14, 20, 24, 26

God made choices when He created: *³God said, "Let there be light... ⁶Let there be a firmament... ⁹Let the waters...be gathered... ¹¹...Let the earth bring forth grass... ¹⁴Let there be lights... ²⁰Let the waters abound... ²⁴Let the earth bring forth the living creature... ²⁶Let Us make man in Our image...let them have dominion..."*

Genesis 6:13–15, 22

Noah made a choice when he built the ark: *¹³And God said to Noah... ¹⁴"Make yourself an ark of gopherwood... ¹⁵And this is how you shall make it...." ²²Thus did Noah, according to all that God commanded him, do did he.*

Exodus 25:1, 8–9, 39:42–43

Moses and the people of Israel made a choice when they built the tabernacle and its furnishings: *¹And the Lord spoke to Moses, saying,... ⁸"And let them make Me a sanctuary; that I may dwell among them. ⁹According to all that I show you, that is, the pattern of the tabernacle and the pattern of all its furnishings, just so you shall make it...."*

⁴²According to all that the Lord had commanded Moses, so the children of Israel did all the work. ⁴³Then Moses looked over all the work, and indeed they had done it; as the Lord had commanded, just so they had done it. And Moses blessed them.

1 Kings 5:5

King Solomon speaking to Hiram, king of Tyre:...*I propose to build a house for the name of the Lord my God, as the Lord spoke to my father*

David, saying, "Your son, whom I will set on your throne in your place, he shall build the house for My name."

4. Man's varied creative abilities demonstrate the uniqueness of each person.

See Chapter 2, Concept 4 for examples of this variety.

5. Man's creativity and his ability to appreciate the creativity of others are affected by sin.

Romans 1:18–20

Sinful man does not see in God's creation what God intends he should see. *¹⁸For the wrath of God is revealed from heaven against all ungodliness... ¹⁹Because what may be known of God is manifest in them, for God has shown it to them. ²⁰For since the creation of the world His invisible attributes are clearly seen, being understood by the things that are made, even His eternal power and Godhead, so that they are without excuse.*

Romans 1:21–24

Because of sin, man's imagination has become empty and his heart darkened, even while man thinks he is wise. *²¹Because although they knew God, they did not glorify Him as God, nor were thankful, but became futile in their thoughts, and their foolish hearts were darkened. ²²Professing to be wise, they became fools.... ²⁴Therefore God also gave them up to uncleanness....*

Romans 1:28–32

When men refuse to acknowledge God, He gives them over to thinking that is depraved or reprobate; the result is that they invent various forms of evil. *²⁸And even as they did not like to retain God in their knowledge, God gave them over to a debased mind, to do those things which are not fitting.... ³⁰inventors of evil things...* [Phillips: *Their minds teemed with diabolical invention;* Amplified Bible: *inventors of new forms of evil*].

Ephesians 2:3

Among whom [i.e., the children of disobedience] *also we all once conducted ourselves* [lifestyle] *in the lusts of our flesh, fulfilling the desires of the flesh and of the mind....*

2 Peter 3:5

Scoffers who do not believe the promise of the Second Coming are ignorant by their own willfulness of God's creative work too. *⁵For this they willfully forget: that by the word of God the heavens were of old....*

2 Kings 16:10–12

An example of the effect of sin on one's appreciation of what he sees: King Ahaz of Israel visited Damascus and saw a heathen altar there that he liked. He sent to Urijah the priest the pattern for it with the details of workmanship. Urijah built a replica and Ahaz used it to replace the brazen altar that God had directed for Israel's use. Here is a perverted love of art that was an offence to God.

III. OUR RESPONSIBILITY

1. We should draw closer to God and understand Him better through studying His creation.

Job 37:14

Elihu speaking to Job: *Listen to this, O Job; stand still and consider the wondrous works of God.*

Job 38–41

In these chapters, God asks questions of Job, calling attention to many of His creations and using them to show His omnipotence and omniscience. Note especially 38:4–6, 16, 19–21, 28–33; 39:19–30; 40:15–23; ch. 41, describing the leviathan.

Job 40:1–5; 42:2–6

Here, Job replies to the Lord in a way that shows that he recognizes God's greatness and his own sinfulness and limited understanding. *¹Moreover the LORD answered Job, and said, ²"Shall the one who contends with the Almighty correct Him? He who rebukes God, let him answer it." ³Then Job answered the LORD, and said, ⁴"Behold, I am vile, what shall I answer You? I lay my hand over my mouth. ⁵Once I have spoken, but I will not answer; yes, twice, but I will proceed no further...."*

⁴²:²I know that You can do everything, and that no purpose of Yours can be withheld from You. ³You asked, "Who is this who hides counsel without knowledge?" Therefore I have uttered what I did not understand, things too wonderful for me, which I did not know. ⁴Listen, please, and let me speak; You said, "I will question you, and you shall answer Me. ⁵I have heard of You by the hearing of the ear, but now my eye sees You. ⁶Therefore I abhor myself, and repent in dust and ashes."

Psalm 8:3–4
³When I consider Your heavens, the work of Your fingers, The moon and the stars, which You have ordained, ⁴What is man, that You are mindful of him, And the son of man that You visit him?

Psalm 19:1–6
¹The heavens declare the glory of God, and the firmament shows His handiwork. ²Day unto day utters speech, and night unto night reveals knowledge. ³There is no speech nor language, where their voice is not heard.

Psalm 104:24–34
Here, the Psalmist describes many aspects of God's creative work. He reacts to these thoughts in the following statements: *²⁴O Lord, how manifold are Your works! In wisdom You have made them all. The earth is full of Your possessions.... ³¹May the glory of the Lord endure forever; May the Lord rejoice in His works.... ³³I will sing to the Lord as long as I live; I will sing praise to my God while I have my being. ³⁴May my meditation be sweet to Him; I will be glad in the Lord.*

See also Romans 1:20; Matthew 6:28–30.

2. We are responsible to think on beautiful things and to appreciate the beauty God has provided.

a. God gives a specific command; we are to respond differently from the world.

Romans 12:2
And do not be conformed to this world, but be transformed by the renewing of your mind, that you may prove what is that good and acceptable and perfect will of God.

Philippians 4:8
Finally, brethren, whatever things are true, whatever things are noble, whatever things are

just, whatever things are pure, whatever things are lovely, whatever things are of good report, if there is any virtue and if there is anything praiseworthy—meditate on these things.

b. God calls to our attention some aspects of His creation that we should think about.

Job 38:22
God speaking to Job: *Have you entered the treasury of snow, or have you seen the treasury of hail?*

Psalm 48:2
Beautiful in elevation, The joy of the whole earth, Is Mount Zion on the sides of the north, The city of the great King.

Ecclesiastes 3:11
He has made every thing beautiful in his time. Also He has put eternity in their hearts, except that no one can find out the work that God does from beginning to end.

Song of Solomon 2:11–13
Solomon's description of Spring: *¹¹For, lo, the winter is past, the rain is over and gone; ¹²The flowers appear on the earth; the time of the singing has come, and the voice of the turtledove is heard in our land; ¹³The fig tree puts forth her green figs, and the vines with the tender grapes give a good smell.*

Matthew 6:28–30
²⁸Consider the lilies of the field, how they grow; they neither toil nor spin, neither do they spin: ²⁹And yet I say to you, that even Solomon in all his glory was not arrayed like one of these.

See also Psalm 8:3–4, 19:1.

3. We must discern between what pleases God and what does not glorify Him; we must ask, "Does this reflect God and His beauty?"

a. God directs that we should specifically seek those things which glorify Him.

Psalm 37:4
Delight yourself also in the Lord; And He shall give you the desires of your heart.

Romans 12:1–2

> *¹Present your bodies a living sacrifice... ²And do not be conformed to this world, but be transformed by the renewing of your mind, that you may prove what is that good and acceptable and perfect will of God.* [Phillips' translation, in verse 2, says: Don't let the world around you squeeze you into its own mold. Philippians 4:8, quoted previously.]

Colossians 3:1–2

> *¹If then you were raised with Christ, seek those things which are above, where Christ is, sitting at the right hand of God. ²Set your mind on things above, not on things on the earth.*

2 Timothy 2:22

> *Flee also youthful lusts: but pursue righteousness, faith, love, peace with those who call on the Lord out of a pure heart.*

b. God also warns us against those things which pollute our minds and hearts, drawing us away from Him.

Romans 13:14

> *But put on the Lord Jesus Christ, and make no provision for the flesh, to fulfill its lusts.*

1 Corinthians 10:23

> *All things are lawful for me, but all things are not helpful, all things are lawful for me, but all things do not edify.*

2 Corinthians 5:17

> *Therefore if anyone is in Christ, he is a new creation, old things have passed away; behold, all things have become new.*

2 Corinthians 7:1

> *Therefore, having these promises, beloved, let us cleanse ourselves from all filthiness of the flesh and spirit, perfecting holiness in the fear of God.*

1 Thessalonians 5:21–22

> *²¹Test all things; hold fast what is good. ²²Abstain from every form of evil.*

2 Timothy 2:4

> *No one engaged in warfare entangles himself with the affairs of this life, that he may please him who enlisted him as a soldier.*

James 1:27

> *Pure religion and undefiled before God and the Father is this,...to keep oneself unspotted from the world.*

1 Peter 2:11

> *Beloved, I beg you as sojourners and pilgrims, abstain from fleshly lusts which war against the soul.*

2 Peter 2:20

> *For if after they have escaped the pollutions of the world through the knowledge of the Lord and Savior Jesus Christ, they are again entangled in them, and overcome, the latter end is worse with them than the beginning.*

1 John 2:15–17

> *¹⁵Do not love the world or the things in the world. If anyone loves the world, the love of the Father is not in him. ¹⁶For all that is in the world, the lust of the flesh, and the lust of the eyes, and the pride of life, is not of the Father, but is of the world. ¹⁷And the world is passing away, and the lust of it; but he who does the will of God abides forever.*

---

4. **We should yield our abilities to God to be used for His glory, whether in enjoyment and appreciation, or in production of that for which He has given us the ability.**

---

a. Statements and examples which apply to every believer.

Psalm 19:14

> *Let the words of my mouth, and the meditation of my heart, be acceptable in Your sight, O LORD, my strength, and my redeemer.*

Psalm 27:4

> The example of David: *One thing I have desired of the LORD, That will I seek: That I may dwell in the house of the LORD All the days of my life, To behold the beauty of the LORD, And to inquire in His temple.*

Psalm 37:4

> *Delight yourself also in the LORD, And He shall give you the desires of your heart.*

Matthew 6:33

But seek first the kingdom of God and His righteousness, and all these things shall be added to you.

1 Corinthians 6:19–20

¹⁹Or do you not know that your body is the temple of the Holy Spirit who is in you, whom you have from God, and you are not your own? ²⁰For you were bought at a price; therefore glorify God in your body and in your spirit, which are God's.

1 Corinthians 10:31

Therefore, whether you eat or drink, or whatever you do, do all to the glory of God.

Colossians 3:17, 23–24

¹⁷And whatever you do in word or deed, do all in the name of the Lord Jesus, giving thanks to God the Father through Him.... ²³And whatever you do, do it heartily, as to the Lord and not to men; ²⁴Knowing that from the Lord you will receive the reward of the inheritance; for you serve the Lord Christ.

Also Colossians 3:1–2; Ezra 7:27, an example which was blessed.

b. Statements concerning yieldedness of special abilities to Him, not the same for all believers.

Matthew 25:14–30; Luke 19:12–26

The parable of the talents, with different dispensations to the various servants, yet the expectation that all would use their gifts for the master's use.

Romans 12:6–8

⁶Having then gifts differing according to the grace that is given to us, let us use them: if prophecy, let us prophesy in proportion to our faith; ⁷Or ministry, let us use it in our ministering; he who teaches, in teaching; ⁸He who exhorts, in exhortation; he who gives, with liberality; he who leads, with diligence; he who shows mercy, with cheerfulness.

1 Peter 4:10–11

¹⁰As each one has received a gift, minister it to one another, as good stewards of the manifold grace of God. ¹¹If anyone speaks, let him speak as the oracles of God. If anyone ministers, let him do it as with the ability which God supplies, that in all things God may be glorified through Jesus Christ, to whom belong the glory and the dominion forever and ever. Amen.

5. We must recognize God's evaluation of physical beauty, whether of the human body or of things, in contrast with spiritual beauty, or beauty of character.

a. The danger of too much emphasis on physical beauty.

Psalm 39:11

The temporariness of beauty accompanied by sin: When with rebukes You correct man for iniquity, You make his beauty melt away like a moth; Surely every man is vapor.

Psalm 49:14

The confinement of physical beauty to this life: Like sheep they [i.e., those who are rich and who build beautiful houses, [vv. 6, 11–12] are laid in the grave; death shall feed on them; The upright shall have dominion over them in the morning; And their beauty shall be consumed in the grave, far from their dwelling.

Proverbs 31:30

Following the description of a virtuous woman: Charm is deceitful and beauty is vain, but a woman who fears the LORD, she shall be praised.

Isaiah 3:16–24

In describing the coming fall of Judah because of God's judgment (v. 1), God describes women decked with all kinds of ornaments and jewelry, and then the end of it all. ²⁴And so it shall be: Instead of a sweet smell there will be a stench; instead of a sash, a rope; instead of well-set hair, baldness; instead of a rich robe, a girding of sackcloth; and branding instead of beauty.

Jeremiah 22:13–17

God sent Jeremiah to King Zedekiah of Judah. Among other things He says: ¹³"Woe to him who builds his house by unrighteousness and his chambers by injustice;... ¹⁴who says, 'I will build myself a wide house with spacious chambers, and cutout windows for it, paneling it with cedar and *painting it with vermilion.' ¹⁵Shall you reign because you enclose yourself in cedar? Did not your father eat and drink, and do justice and righteousness? Then it was well with him?"*

Ezekiel 28:12–19

A description that goes beyond the king of Tyre to Satan, showing his original beauty, his pride, and God's promised judgment: *¹²Thus says the LORD God: "You were the seal of perfection, full of wisdom and perfect in beauty. ¹³You were in Eden, the garden of God; every precious stone was your covering: the sardius, topaz, and diamond, beryl, onyx, and jasper, sapphire, turquoise, and emerald with gold. The workmanship of your timbrels and pipes was prepared for you on the day you were created.... ¹⁷Your heart was lifted up because of your beauty; you corrupted your wisdom for the sake of your splendor; I cast you to the ground, I laid you before kings, that they might gaze at you."*

Matthew 23:27

Jesus' warning against mere outward beauty: *Woe to you, scribes and Pharisees, hypocrites! For you are like whitewashed tombs which indeed appear beautiful outwardly, but inside are full of dead men's bones and all uncleanness.*

1 Timothy 2:9–10

⁹In like manner also, that the women adorn themselves in modest apparel, with propriety and moderation, not with braided hair or gold or pearls or costly clothing; ¹⁰But which is proper for women professing godliness, with good works.

1 Peter 3:3–6

[Wives] ³Do not let your beauty be that outward adorning of arranging the hair, of wearing gold, or of putting on fine apparel; ⁴But let it be the hidden person of the heart, with the incorruptible ornament of a gentle and quiet spirit, which is very precious in the sight of God.

b. The importance of spiritual beauty, the beauty of a holy life.

1 Chronicles 16:29

Part of the psalm of thanksgiving by David at the return of the ark to Jerusalem: *Give to the LORD the glory due His name; bring an offering, and come before Him. Oh, worship the LORD in the beauty of holiness.*

2 Chronicles 20:21

Jehoshaphat, after God promised victory over enemies, commanded praise to the Lord. And when he had consulted with the people, he appointed those who should sing to the LORD, and who should praise the beauty of holiness, as they went out before the army and were saying: *"Praise the LORD, for His mercy endures forever."*

Psalm 90:17

And let the beauty of the LORD our God be upon us: And establish the work of our hands for us; Yes, establish the work of our hands.

Psalm 96:9

O worship the LORD in the beauty of holiness! Tremble before Him, all the earth.

Isaiah 52:7; also Romans 10:15

A recognition of the beauty of the bringing of God's message: *How beautiful upon the mountains are the feet of him who brings good news, who proclaims peace, who brings glad tidings of good things, who proclaims salvation, who says to Zion, "Your God reigns!"* [In Isaiah referring to the Kingdom, in Romans to the preaching of the Gospel.]

See also Proverbs 31:30; 1 Timothy 2:9–10; 1 Peter 3:36; all of which are quoted in the preceding section.

"In a small way human creative hands imitate this profusion of God, going beyond the minimum requirements of getting the job done. Creative hands are not content to spread on the frosting; they must make a tasteful arrangement of swirls and color. They don't just apply a coat of varnish; they polish the surface until it glows like satin. Creative hands do more than plant seeds; they place them in a tasteful and eye-pleasing garden arrangement."
—LeRoy Koopman, Source unknown.

"For the Christian, God is the supreme artist....God looked at His creation as it progressed and saw that it was good; when He had completed it, He saw it was 'very good.'...The Great Artist was evidently much pleased with His world. It was a world filled with wonderful objects, shapes, and movements, a world abundant in rich colors like those of the rainbow and the rose, rich textures like those of beaver fur and magnolia leaves, rich odors like those of the quince and the honeysuckle, rich sounds like those of thunder and running streams, and rich tastes like those of watermelon and chocolate."
—Clyde S. Kilby, *Christianity and Aesthetics*, p. 18.

"If God made the flowers, they are worth painting and writing about. If God made the birds, they are worth painting. If God made the sky, the sky is worth painting. If God made the ocean, indeed it's worth writing poetry about. It is worth man's while to create works upon the basis of the great works God has already created."
—Francis A. Schaeffer, *Art and the Bible*, p. 60.

Arts & Crafts

[Fine Arts/Health]

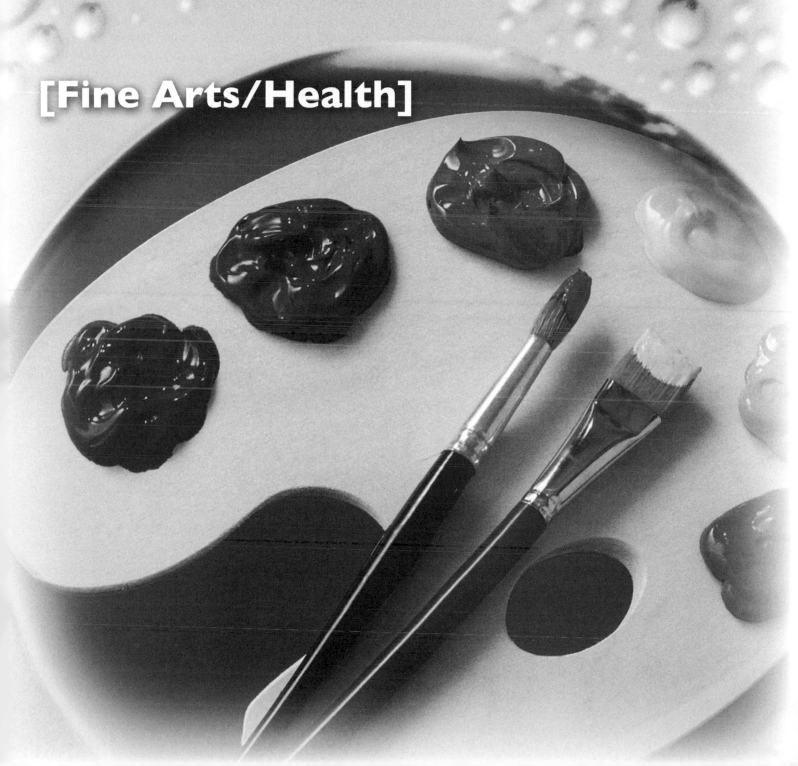

Arts & Crafts:
Biblical Concepts/Background

1. God is interested in beauty.

2. God is pleased with art which includes both religious and nonreligious subjects.

3. God does not spare cost when expensive materials are needed to produce art which portrays His message.

4. God gives a variety of artistic abilities.

5. God will use the various artistic talents He gives, as we submit to Him.

6. God calls attention to specific creative works of His that are worthy of our attention and meditation.

7. Works of art may portray a variety of messages, and may be used for both good and evil purposes.

   a. Therefore, the message and the use to which an art work is put must be judged on the basis of the Word of God.

   b. Therefore, the fact that a work of art is well executed does not guarantee the truth of the message, or the worthiness of its use.

8. No object created by man or God is to become an object of worship.

Many of the concepts presented in Chapter 1, "Creativity," are relevant to the representational arts included in this section.

1. God is interested in beauty.

Genesis 1–2

God created the earth, the heavens, and everything in the earth. Then He declared it all very good. In the Garden He made *trees pleasant to the sight,* as well as *good for food.* His purpose was not completely utilitarian. (2:9)

Exodus 25:1–9

When the Lord directed Moses to take an offering for the building of a sanctuary for Him, He listed the items people were to bring. They included much that was beyond the necessities of worship: gold and silver and brass, colorful cloth and skins, spices and incense, precious stones.

Exodus 25:9 through Chapter 27

God gave the pattern; it was not of man's own ingenuity. *⁹According to all that I show you, that is, the pattern of the tabernacle and the pattern of all its furnishings, just so you shall make it.* Many details were spelled out. The ark, made of wood, was *to be overlaid with gold;* so were the staves or rods by which it was to be carried. The mercy seat was to be pure gold, holding two cherubims of hammered gold. The table for the shewbread could have been only wood, but it too was covered with gold, and with a gold rim or border around the edge. The dishes, spoons and bowls used were to be pure gold. The candlestick was to be of hammered gold, decorated with almond flowers and leaves. The curtains closing the tabernacle, and those separating the holy place from the holy of holies were to be colorful. Even the boards that made the sides of the building itself were to be covered with gold, standing in silver sockets.

Exodus 28

God's command to Moses was that the garments of the high priest were to be made *for glory and for beauty* (vv. 2, 40). Note in the verses which follow: the coat was to be embroidered (vv. 4, 39), the materials were to be gold, blue, purple, and scarlet, and fine linen; there were to be engraved stones (vv. 9–12); twelve stones set in gold and with names engraved were to decorate the breastplate (vv. 15–22); the robe was to be blue, trimmed with pomegranates and bells around the hem; the crown or mitre was to be engraved gold.

> *Note: Dr. Francis Schaeffer points out the fact that the pomegranates were to be of blue, purple, and scarlet. Blue is not a natural color of a pomegranate; all art need not be realistic.*
> *—Art and the Bible* (Inter–Varsity Press, 1976), p. 14.

1 Chronicles 28:11–12, 19

The pattern for the temple that Solomon built came from God; it was an elegant temple! *[11]Then David gave his son Solomon the plans for the vestibule... [12]And the plans for all that he had by the Spirit... [19]All this, said David, the L*ORD *made me understand in writing by His hand upon me, all the works of these plans.*

PROJECT: Study 1 Kings 6–7; 1 Chronicles 28:11–19; 29:1–8; 2 Chronicles 2–4. List the various kinds of art work included in the temple of Solomon. Note the use of metals, stones, engraving, carving. Note also the various items pictured, both from nature and from the angelic realm.

Proverbs 31:21–22, 24

The virtuous woman described by God clothed her household in scarlet; she dressed herself in tapestry, made of silk and purple; she made and sold fine linens in the marketplace.

---

2. God is pleased with art which includes both religious and nonreligious subjects.

Exodus 25–27

In the tabernacle built to God's command were representations of cherubims on the mercy seat, the linen covering that was over the top, and on the veil that closed in the holy of holies. On the candlestick were almond blossoms and calyxes in gold, alternating on the branches.

Exodus 28:33–34

On the hem of the high priest's robe were alternating golden bells and pomegranates.

2 Chronicles 3:3–4:5

When Solomon built the temple according to the plan given to David, he overlaid the ceiling with gold on which were designs of palm trees and chains (v. 5); he engraved cherubims on the walls (v. 7); he made two three-dimensional cherubims for the most holy house (vv. 10–13); he made pomegranates to decorate the chains which hung from the 52–foot pillars in front of the temple; he encircled the molten sea with ten figures of oxen, and rested the huge sea on twelve more

oxen, three facing in each direction (4:2–4); he decorated the brim with lilies (4:5). 1 Kings 7:29, 36 mentions also lions, oxen, palm trees, and cherubim.

Ezekiel 4:1

God commanded the prophet Ezekiel to draw the city of Jerusalem on a tile. With this as a background he was to dramatize a message to Israel.

---

3. God does not spare cost when expensive materials are needed to produce art which portrays His message.

Exodus 25:3–7 and following

Note the kinds of offerings which God asked of his people who had for many years been slaves in Egypt. It is true that, when they were delivered from Egypt, they asked and received clothing and jewels of silver and gold (12:35–36); it would have been easy for them to feel that these things were for their own use. Yet God asked for them, and they gave in abundance (35:4–29).

1 Chronicles 28:14–18; 29:2–5

David lists all that he gave for the temple which would be built after he was gone, and says that all of this was directed by God (29:19).

1 Chronicles 29:6–9

The princes under David, along with the people, willingly and joyfully made offerings to God for the future temple.

2 Chronicles 2:4–9

Solomon sent to Hiram, King of Tyre, for materials and craftsmen who would be able to assist in building so great a temple. He recognized the magnitude of his undertaking (vv. 5–6). Read the following chapters to appreciate the elegance and great cost of this temple, built according to God's directions.

---

4. God gives a variety of artistic abilities.

For Scriptures which show God's specific endowment of certain named persons, see Chapter 1, I, concept 6. In the references which follow, a variety of artisans are mentioned, indicating that they were active in Bible times.

Carving

1 Kings 6:18, 29, 32, 35

The woodwork of the temple was decorated with carvings, some of which were overlaid with gold. See also 2 Chr. 3:5, 7; Psa. 74:6–7; Exodus 31:5; 35:33.

Proverbs 7:16

Here, a prostitute is telling of her elegant bed decorated with carvings from Egypt—a God–given ability misused.

Drawing

Ezekiel 4:1

God's command to Ezekiel to draw a picture of Jerusalem to convey a message of judgment to Israel.

Dyeing

Exodus 25:5, 26:14

One of the gifts which God asked from the Israelites during the wilderness journey was skins of rams, dyed red, to be used in the tabernacle construction.

Isaiah 63:1

Dyed garments from Edom are mentioned here.

Engraving

Exodus 32:4

Aaron used an engraving tool to work upon the cast form of the golden calf.

Exodus 28:9–11, 21.

The names of the tribes of Israel were to be engraved on onyx stones, one for each shoulder of the high priest. Likewise, one tribe's name was to be engraved on each of twelve stones as part of the breastplate. See also 39:6–14.

Exodus 28:36–38, 39:30

The words *Holiness to the Lord* were engraved on a gold plate fastened to the mitre which the high priest wore.

Lapidary

Exodus 31:5, 35:33

Part of the work for which God gave Bezaleel special ability was the cutting of stones.

Exodus 28:9–21; 39:6–14

Important in the making of the breastplate and the ephod for the high priest.

2 Samuel 1:30; 1 Chronicles 20:2

Stones were used in kings' crowns.

Needlework, embroidery

Exodus 26:1, 31, 36; 27:16

Cherubim embroidered on the curtains that covered the tabernacle, and on the veil in front of the holy of holies; needlework of some kind on the outer veil at the entrance to the tabernacle.

Exodus 28:4, 39

The high priest's coat was to be embroidered. Needlework was frequently used on the garments of important people: e.g., Judges 5:30, on the garments of Sisera, the captain of the army of the Canaanites; Ezekiel 26:16, on garments of the princes of Tyre; Psalm 45:14, on the dress of the daughter of Tyre who was to be Solomon's bride.

Pottery

1 Chronicles 4:23

Here, among the posterity of Judah listed in the official genealogies were potters. *23These were the potters, and those who dwell at Netaim and Gederah; there they dwelt with the king for his work.*

Isaiah 29:16

In warning Judah of coming judgment, God refers to the submission of clay to the potter: *16Surely you have things turned around! Shall the potter be esteemed as the clay; for shall the thing made say of him who made it, "He did not make me"? Or shall the thing formed say of him who formed it, "He has no understanding?"*

Jeremiah 18:1–6

Jeremiah's visit to the potter's house at the command of the Lord.

Spinning, weaving, tapestry–making

Exodus 26:1–13, 31, 36

Hangings for the tabernacle. See also Exodus 27:9–16, 36:8–18.

Exodus 35:25–26.

Women whose heart stirred with wisdom, spun yarn for the tabernacle curtains, using blue, purple, scarlet, fine linen, and goats' hair.

Exodus 39:1–3, 8, 22, 27

Service cloths and garments for Aaron

were made of woven materials, using the yarns listed above, plus fine threads made of beaten gold (v. 3). See also 28:32.

Esther 1:6

Tapestries were used in the palace in Shushan: *6There were white and blue linen curtains fastened with cords of fine linen and purple on silver rods and marble pillars....*

1 Kings 23:7; Proverbs 7:16

Tapestry was used for evil purposes, in idolatrous groves, and by prostitutes to decorate their beds.

Proverbs 31:22

The virtuous woman is described as having coverings of tapestry, silk, and purple. See also Isaiah 19:9, 38:12.

5. God will use the various artistic talents He gives, as we submit to Him.

Exodus 31:2–6, 35:30–35, 36:1–8.

Here are the accounts of the work of Bezaleel, Aholiab, and those who worked and learned under them. Note several emphases: (1) God filled them with His Spirit, which resulted in wisdom, understanding, knowledge, workmanship; (2) God gave wisdom to those who were already wise-hearted (31:6, 36:2); (3) God's enablement showed itself in a great variety of specialized crafts, along with the teaching of those crafts. See also 39:32–43 (especially vv. 32, 42–43).

1 Kings 7:13, 14; 2 Chronicles 2:7, 13–14

When Solomon set about to build the temple, he sent to Hiram, King of Tyre, for a skillful man who would be able to do a variety of crafts and who could also work with his own skilled laborers. King Hiram sent a craftsman, also named Hiram (or Huram); his description indicates "a man who could do anything." Note the expanse of his abilities: *cunning, endued with understanding, skilled to work in gold and silver, bronze and iron, stone and wood, purple and blue, fine linen and crimson, and to make any engraving and to accomplish any plan which may be given to him,* able to work with Solomon's skilled men and with those appointed by David. Though we do not know craftsman Hiram's spiritual state, he went at the request of Hiram his king who was eager to be of assistance to Solomon. He apparently was willing to be used in this project.

Ecclesiastes 9:10

Whatever your hand finds to do, do it with your might; for there is no work or device or knowledge or wisdom in the grave where you are going.

Matthew 25:14–30; Luke 19:11–27

Parables of the talents and the pounds.

Romans 6:13

And do not present your members as instruments of unrighteousness to sin, but present yourselves to God as being alive from the dead, and your members as instruments of righteousness to God.

Romans 12:1

I beseech you therefore, brethren, by the mercies of God, that you present your bodies a living sacrifice, holy, acceptable to God, which is your reasonable service.

1 Corinthians 6:19–20

19Or do you not know that your body is the temple of the Holy Spirit who is in you, whom you have from God, and you are not your own? 20For you were bought at a price; therefore glorify God in your body and in your spirit, which are God's.

1 Corinthians 10:31

Therefore, whether you eat or drink, or whatever you do, do all to the glory of God.

Colossians 3:22–23

22Servants, obey in all things your masters according to the flesh, not with eye service, as men-pleasers, but in sincerity of heart, fearing God, 23And whatever you do, do it heartily, as to the Lord and not to men.

6. God calls attention to specific creative works of His that are worthy of our attention and meditation.

Psalm 1:3

The picture of a healthy tree, drinking up nourishment and bearing fruit.

Job 38–41

Here, God asks Job a long series of questions in which He rehearses some of the wonders of His creation. Job realizes his own limitations as never before. See Job 42:5–6.

Psalm 8:3–4

³When I consider Your heavens, the work of Your fingers, The moon and the stars, which You have ordained; ⁴What is man, that You are mindful of him, And the son of man that You visit him?

Psalm 19:1

The heavens declare the glory of God; and the firmament shows His handiwork.

See also Psalms 65:9–13; 104:1–10, 13; 136:5–9.

---

7. Works of art may portray a variety of messages, and may be used for both good and evil purposes.

---

a. Therefore, the message and the use to which an art work is put must be judged on the basis of the Word of God.

b. Therefore, the fact that a work of art is well executed does not guarantee the truth of the message, or the worthiness of its use.

Examples:

The use of objects of art as idols: Exodus 32:2–6; Deuteronomy 7:5; Isaiah 44:9–21, 45:20; Habakkuk 2:18–19; 2 Kings 21:7—Manasseh set a graven image (NASB: *a carved image of Asherah*) in the temple set apart for the Lord; 1 Chronicles 11:14–15—Jeroboam ordained priests for the worship of satyrs (*devils,* in KJV) and calves which he had made.

The use of art works—tapestry, carved works, and fine linen—to decorate the bed of a prostitute: Proverbs 7:16 and 1 Kings 23:7.

---

8. No object created by man or God is to become an object of worship.

Exodus 20:4–5. (The original commandment); also 34:13–14.

⁴You shall not make for yourself any carved image, or any likeness of anything that is in heaven above, or that is in the earth beneath, or that is in the water under the earth. ⁵You shall not bow down to them nor serve them. For I, the LORD your God, am a jealous God....

Leviticus 26:1

You shall not make idols for yourselves; neither a carved image nor a sacred pillar shall you rear up for yourselves, nor shall you set up an engraved stone in your land, to bow down to it; for I am the LORD your God.

Deuteronomy 4:15–19

Spoken to the new generation: *¹⁵Take careful heed to yourselves, for you saw no form [NASB: you did not see any form] when the LORD spoke to you at Horeb out of the midst of the fire; ¹⁶Lest you act corruptly and make for yourselves a carved image in the form of any figure: the likeness of male or female, ¹⁷The likeness of any beast that is on the earth, or the likeness of any winged bird... ¹⁸of anything that creeps...of any fish.... ¹⁹And take heed, lest you lift your eyes to heaven, and when you see the sun, the moon, and the stars, all the host of heaven, you feel driven to worship them and serve them...* (See also 27:15.)

2 Kings 18:14

In the revival under King Hezekiah, he not only broke down the various images and groves which had been constructed for worship, but he also broke up the brazen serpent which Moses had made at God's command. It had now become an object of worship and therefore no longer served any godly purpose.

"Beauty is God's handwriting."
—Anne Louise Flint, in *God in the Classroom,* Marjorie Adams, ed., p. 62.

"In our traditional view of art, in folk art, Christian and Oriental art, there is no essential distinction of a fine or useless art from a utilitarian craftsmanship. There is no distinction in principle of orator from carpenter, but only a distinction of things well and truly made from things not so made and of what is beautiful from what is ugly..."
—Amanda Coomaraswamy, *Christian and Oriental Philosophy of Art* (N.Y.: Dover Publications), p. 27.

Music

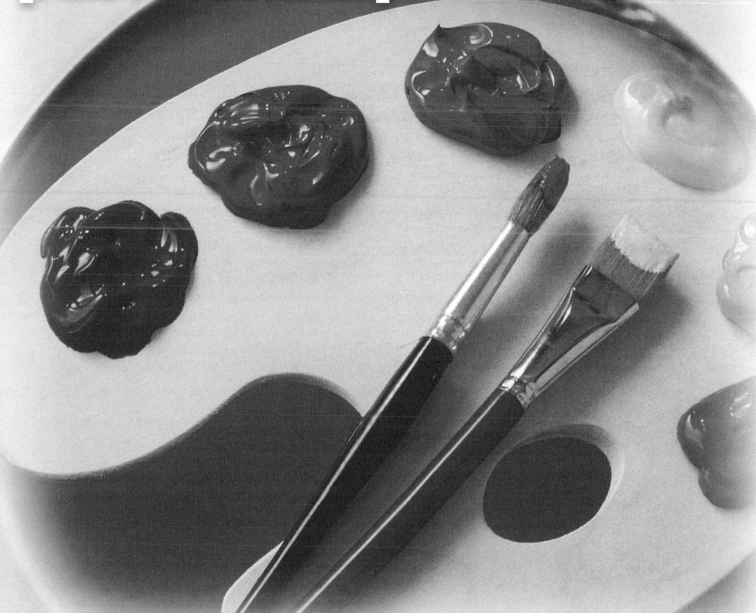

Music:
Biblical Concepts

I. THE GIFT OF MUSIC

1. Music is characteristic of heaven.
2. Music is everywhere in the universe to praise God.
3. Music is God's gift to us.
   a. God made man's voice, the most complex of instruments.
   b. God gave man the ability to invent musical instruments.
   c. God made the materials from which instruments are made.
   d. God established the principles by which sound works, and which govern music.
   e. God enables men to write music and words; "God giveth a song."
   f. God made man with a responsiveness to music.
   g. A revival in music often accompanies revival of heart toward God.
4. Music appeared early in the history of man and has been an important part of every known culture of every age.
5. Musicians and music teachers have had a long history in serving God.

II. THE FUNCTIONS OF MUSIC

1. The major scriptural function of music is for the praise and worship of God—a vertical function.
   a. The Bible is full of examples of the use of music in worship, especially in the Old Testament.
   b. Many Biblical saints stated their personal praise to God by way of music.
   c. Believers of every age are encouraged to express praise in music.
2. Music has a rightful place in the commemoration of historical events, the celebration of victories and other special occasions.
3. Music may express faith in God, to which He responds in giving victory.
4. Music is a method of teaching, admonishing, exhorting, and rebuking.
5. Music is a means of communication among people—a horizontal function.
   a. Music serves as a signal or alarm, or call to assembly. The trumpet and horn are especially significant for this use.
   b. Music serves to refresh, to encourage, to provide enjoyment for both the performer and the listener.
6. Music serves as an outlet for various emotions.
7. Music may be unacceptable with God because of its evil purpose or its insincerity.

III. THE PERFORMANCE AND APPRECIATION OF MUSIC

1. Both vocal and instrumental music may be used in the worship of the Lord.
2. A variety of musical instruments have been used in bringing praise to the Lord; some of the same instruments have also been used for evil.
3. A variety of sacred music is encouraged and exemplified in the Bible.
4. Music and art have frequently been combined in times of worship and celebration.
5. The beliefs, attitudes, and goals of men are reflected in the music they produce and use, or by their lack of disposition to music.
   a. The lack of disposition to music often indicates sadness, depression, or God's judgment.
   b. The kind of music one produces, or with which he identifies, depends on his own inner thoughts and view of life.
6. Our use of music should be for the glory of God and should be tempered by its effect on others and our concern for them.

Music:
Biblical Concepts/Background

7. The sounds in music must be distinct and the words intelligible if listeners are to receive the message.

8. Singers should understand what they are singing and experience the truth expressed.

9. God is pleased with excellence in musical performance which is done for His glory.

10. The use of music for sinful purposes displeases God and will be judged.

VALUES OF MUSIC IN A
CHRISTIAN SCHOOL

1. *To give enjoyment.*
2. *To help children achieve successes.*
3. *To encourage participation and social development.*
4. *To develop tolerance, both as listeners and performers.*
5. *To develop self–discipline.*
6. *To teach communication without words.*
7. *To create a sense of serenity.*
8. *To teach discernment.*
9. *To acquaint with other cultures and historical periods.*
10. *To bring glory to God.*
—Adapted from Heather Greenwood, "Why Include Music in the Christian School Curriculum?" *Nurture* (Australia), Autumn, 1981.

WHAT IS MUSIC?

"Music is the harmonious voice of creation; an echo of the invisible world; one note of the divine concord which the entire universe is destined one day to sound."
—Giuseppe Mazzini (1805–1872), Italian patriot.

"There is something marvelous in music. I might almost say it is, in itself, a marvel. Its position is somewhere between the region of thought and that of phenomena; a glimmering medium between mind and matter, related to both and yet differing from either. Spiritual and yet requiring rhythm; material and yet independent of space."
—Heinrich Heine (1797–1856), German poet.

"Music is the fourth great material want of our nature—first food, then raiment, then shelter, then music."
—Christian Nestell Bovee (1820–1904), American author and editor.

"Music is one of the fairest and most glorious gifts of God, to which Satan is a bitter enemy, for it removes from the heart the weight of sorrow, and the fascination of evil thoughts."
—Martin Luther (1483–1546), German reformer.

Music is a bridge through time. "I can hear what the songs of the birds were like as they sang before man ever sang a song. Bird song: an element of continuity with the time before man and woman were there to hear them. Bird songs, heard by God and the angels. Our ears can hear bird songs that were heard by Adam and Eve, by Abraham and Isaac, by David and Daniel, by Luther and Calvin, Spurgeon and Livingstone."
—Edith Schaeffer, "Music: A Bridge through Time." *Christianity Today*, June 17, 1977.

Much of the material of Chapter I has application to music and should therefore be studied along with these more specific concepts.

I. THE GIFT OF MUSIC

1. Music is characteristic of heaven.

In the Old Testament

Psalms and songs commemorating a particular event, such as Exodus 15, Judges 5, Psalm 105:23–39, 106:7–33 *were created.* See footnote in *Scofield Reference Bible.* This goes back to the time of the creation of Satan, or Lucifer, the son of the morning.

Zephaniah 3:17

God speaking of Israel in the Kingdom: *He will rejoice over you with singing. God sings!*

1 Corinthians 15:52

When the Lord returns for His own, the signal is represented as a musical one: *52In a moment, in the twinkling of an eye, at the last trump. For the trumpet will sound, and the dead will be raised incorruptible, and we shall be changed.*

1 Thessalonians 4:16–17

Here again is the description of the coming Rapture of believers, with the musical accompaniment: *16For the Lord Himself will descend from heaven with a shout, with the voice of an archangel, and with the trumpet of God. And the dead in Christ will rise first: 17...to meet the Lord in the air...*

Hebrews 2:9, 12

9But we see Jesus... 12Saying, "I will declare Your name to My brethren; in the midst of the congregation I will sing praise to You."

> *"It is our happy privilege as priests to sing praise unto God, to offer up worship and thanksgiving to Him, but is it wondrous to listen...to Him who is the Priest and Psalmist, whose theme is ever, as it was here upon earth, the Father's name and the Father's glory...Listen to Him, the risen Lord, in the midst of those whom now He can own as His brethren, declaring the glory of God's name, and then lifting up His own high-priestly, mighty voice, leading the praises of His people in all the joy of exultant worship, pouring out His heart in leading the praises of his people in worship..."*
> —S. Ridout, *Lectures on the Epistle to the Hebrews* (N.Y.: Loizeaux, 1947), p. 45.

Revelation 5:8–9

A future scene in heaven: *8Now when He had taken the scroll, the four living creatures and the twenty-four elders fell down before the Lamb... 9And they sang a new song, saying, "You are worthy..."*

Revelation 14:2–3

2And I heard a voice from heaven, like the voice of many waters, and like the voice of loud thunder. And I heard the sound of harpists playing their harps: 3And they sang as it were a new song before the throne, before the four living creatures, and the elders; and no one could learn that song except the hundred and forty-four thousand who were redeemed from the earth.

Revelation 15:2–3

2And I saw something like a sea of glass mingled with fire, and those who have the victory over the beast, over his image and over his mark and over the number of his name, standing on the sea of glass, having harps of God. 3And they sing the song of Moses, the servant of God, and the song of the Lamb, saying: "Great and marvelous are Your works, Lord God Almighty! Just and true are Your ways, O King of the saints."

See also Revelation 4:8, 11, 19:6–7.

2. Music is everywhere in the universe to praise God.

Exodus 15:2

The testimony of Moses and Israel after the Red Sea: The Lord is the song of his people. *2The LORD is my strength and song, and He has become my salvation....*

1 Chronicles 16:23, 33

David praising God after the return of the Ark: *23Sing to the LORD, all the earth; proclaim the good news of His salvation from day to day.... 33Then the trees of the woods shall rejoice before the LORD, for He is coming to judge the earth.*

Job 38:4–7

Music at Creation: *4Where were you when I laid the foundations of the earth? Tell Me, if you have understanding, 5Who determined its measurements? Surely you know! Or who stretched the line upon it? 6To what were its foundations fastened? Or who laid its cornerstone; 7When the* morning stars sang together, and all the sons of God shouted for joy?*

Psalm 65:13

After a recital of God's blessings on the earth: *[13]The pastures are clothed with flocks; The valleys also are covered with grain; They shout for joy, they also sing.*

Psalm 104:12

The Psalmist speaks of the blessings of streams and springs that provide for animals and birds: *[12]By them [springs] the birds of the heavens have their habitation; They sing among the branches.*

Song of Solomon 2:12

Solomon's description of Spring: *[12]The flowers appear on the earth, the time of the singing has come, and the voice of the turtledove is heard in our land.*

Isaiah 44:23

All nature to praise God for his redemption of Israel: *[23]Sing, O heavens, for the LORD has done it! Shout, you lower parts of the earth; break forth into singing, you mountains, O forest, and every tree in it! for the LORD has redeemed Jacob, and glorified Himself in Israel.*

Zephaniah 3:17

Again, God rejoicing over Israel in the Kingdom: *[17]The LORD your God in your midst, the Mighty One, will save; He will rejoice over you with gladness, He will quiet you in His love, He will rejoice over you with singing.*

Ephesians 5:18–19

Singing, the result of a Spirit filled life: *[18]Be filled with the Spirit; [19]Speaking to one another in psalms and hymns and spiritual songs, singing and making melody in your heart to the Lord.* (See also Psalm 40:3.)

Colossians 3:16

Let the word of Christ dwell in you richly in all wisdom; teaching and admonishing one another in psalms and hymns and spiritual songs, singing with grace in your hearts to the Lord.

James 5:13

Is anyone among you...cheerful? Let him sing psalms.

> *"Yea, music is the prophet's art; Among the gifts that God hath sent, One of the most magnificent."*
> —Henry Wadsworth Longfellow (1807-1882).

---

3. Music is God's gift to us.

a. God made man's voice, the most complex of instruments.

Exodus 4:11

God speaking to Moses: *So the LORD said to him, "Who has made man's mouth?... Have not I the LORD?"*

Genesis 2:19–24

God gave man the ability to speak in the beginning, and expected him to speak: *[19] Out of the ground the LORD God formed every beast of the field and every bird of the air, and brought them to Adam to see what he would call them. And whatever Adam called each living creature, that was its name. [20]So Adam gave names to all cattle, to the birds of the air, and to every beast of the field. But for Adam there was not found a helper comparable to him. [21]And the LORD God... [22]He made into a woman, and He brought her to the man. [23]And Adam said, "This is now bone of my bones and flesh of my flesh; she shall be called Woman, because she was taken out of Man."*

b. God gave man the ability to invent musical instruments.

Examples:

Genesis 4:21

Jubal is described as the father of all such as handle the harp and the organ (NASB: *the lyre and the pipe*).

1 Chronicles 23:5

David was responsible for the making of instruments for 4,000 Levite musicians: *[5]Four thousand praised the LORD with musical instruments, "which I made," said David, "for giving praise."* (See also 2 Chronicles 7:6, 29:26; Amos 6:5.)

1 Kings 10:12

Solomon also was involved in making harps and psalteries for his singers. See also 2 Chron. 9:11, using algum trees (probably red sandalwood) imported from Tyre.

c. God made the materials from which instruments are made.

d. God established the principles by which sound works, and which govern music.

Colossians 1:16–17

16For by Him all things were created...all things were created through Him and for Him: 17And He is before all things and in Him all things consist [or hold together].

e. God enables men to write music and words; "God giveth a song."

Exodus 15:1–21

The song sung by Moses and Israel in celebration of the safe crossing of the Red Sea and the destruction of their Egyptian followers; obviously written for the occasion.

Deuteronomy 31:19–22, 30, and 32:1–44.

God, in giving Moses warnings to convey to the people of Israel, says: *19Now therefore, write down this song for yourselves, and teach it to the children of Israel; put it in their mouths, that this song may be a witness for Me against the children of Israel. 20When I have brought them to the land flowing with milk and honey, of which I swore to their fathers, and they have eaten and filled themselves and grown fat, then they will turn to other gods and serve them; and they will provoke Me and break My covenant. 21Then it shall be, when many evils and troubles have come upon them, that this song will testify against them as a witness; for it will not be forgotten in the mouths of their descendants.... 22Therefore Moses wrote this song the same day, and taught it to the children of Israel.* 32:1–44 gives the song. Not only did Moses write it, but God commanded it.

Judges 5

The song sung by Deborah and Barak in celebration of Israel's victory over the Canaanites who had oppressed them. The song reviews some of the history of the nation, but also relates to the specific occasion.

2 Samuel 1:17–27

David's song of lament over the death of Saul and Jonathan.

1 Chronicles 16:7–36

The occasion was the bringing of the ark of God to Jerusalem, and there was great celebration and praise to God (vv. 1–6). *7And on that day David first delivered this psalm into the hand of Asaph and his brethren* (David's choir directors). Verses 8–36 give the song.

1 Kings 4:29–32

In response to Solomon's request for wisdom to rule and judge his people, God gave wisdom in other areas as well. *29And God gave Solomon wisdom exceedingly great understanding, and largeness of heart like the sand on the seashore.... 32He spoke three thousand proverbs, and his songs were one thousand and five.* [Quite a songwriter!]

Isaiah 38:9–20

Hezekiah's song after his life was spared by God, with the accompaniment of stringed instruments (v. 20).

Job 35:10

Elihu, in speaking to Job, recognizes God as the one who gives songs in the night. *10...Where is God my Maker, Who gives songs in the night...*

Psalm 40:3

David, in testimony concerning what God does for one who trusts Him says: *3He has put a new song in my mouth—Praise to our God; Many will see it and fear, And will trust in the LORD.*

The Book of Psalms

Here is a book full of the songs. Based on the titles given them in the Hebrew Bible, 73 are ascribed to David, 12 to Asaph, 10 to sons of Korah, 2 to Solomon, one to Heman, one to Ethan, and one to Moses. Twelve are anonymous.

The fact that many of the Psalms are addressed *To the chief Musician* indicates that they were to be sung, not merely quoted as poems. Also the frequent reference to accompanying instruments, given in the headings further adds to this emphasis. One example is *Neginoth,* which appears at the beginning of Psalms 3, 5, 53–54, 60, 66, 75, and means "stringed instruments."

Since David wrote more of the Psalms than others, his qualifications for songwriting are of interest:

1) *Skilled as a musician. 1 Sam. 16:17–18; Amos 6:5.*
2) *Able as a poet. 2 Sam. 1:19–27.*
3) *Filled with deep feeling and rich imagination. 2 Sam. 18:33.*
4) *Trusting and worshiping God. 1 Kgs. 11:4, 14:8.*
5) *Varied in his experience in life— shepherd, warrior, leader, king, administrator, musician, writer, poet, parent, sinner, spiritual giant.*
6) *Endued in a special way with the Spirit of God. 2 Sam. 23:1–2.*

—Adapted from Karl Smith, *Our Refuge and Strength:* Adult Student. (Des Plaines, IL: Regular Baptist Press, 1965)

---

f. God made man with a responsiveness to music.

Exodus 32:17–19

Moses and Joshua, descending from the mount, recognized the music for what it was and responded accordingly, condemning the sin of idolatrous worship of the golden calf. The people also had responded to the music, *rising up to play* (v. 6).

1 Samuel 16:23

And so it was, whenever the spirit from God was upon Saul, that David would take a harp and play it with his hand. Then Saul would become refreshed and well, and the distressing spirit would depart from him.

Acts 16:25–34

When Paul and Silas prayed and sang praises to God in the jail at Philippi, the prisoners heard them. In spite of the open door, due to the earthquake, no prisoner left.

g. A revival in music often accompanies revival of heart toward God.

Examples:

2 Chronicles 15:8–15
Revival under Asa.

2 Chronicles 20:3–30
Revival under Jehoshaphat.

2 Chronicles 23:16–21
Revival under Joash and Jehoida.

2 Chronicles 29:3–36 (Esp. vv. 25–36)
Revival under Hezekiah.

2 Chronicles 34:8–13 and 35:1–19
Revival under Josiah.

Nehemiah 12:35–47
Revival under Nehemiah after the building of the walls of Jerusalem.

PROJECT: Examine this principle as it relates to more modern revivals. Study the importance and use of music in the ministries of such persons as Luther, the Wesleys, George Whitefield, Jonathan Edwards, Dwight L. Moody.

"What I wish is to make hymns for the people, that the Word of God may dwell in their hearts by means of songs also."
—Martin Luther.

---

4. **Music appeared early in the history of man and has been an important part of every known culture of every age.**

Genesis 4:21

Here is reference to Jubal, called *the father of all such as handle the harp and organ.* See Chapter 1, I, Concept 7 for his identity and ancestry.

Genesis 31:27

Here, Laban scolds Jacob for leaving without notice, lamenting the lack of opportunity for the usual musical farewell. *[27]Why did you flee away secretly, and steal away from me, and not tell me; for I might have sent you away with joy and songs, with timbrel and harp?*

Ezra 2:65

Here among the returning remnant of Israel are mentioned 200 singing men and women. These are believed not to have been the temple singers, but rather professional entertainers used at banquets, feasts and funerals. They evidently learned their music while captives in Babylon and Assyria.

The Poetical Books of the Old Testament

This great section of the Bible, along with the Books of Chronicles and many other specific passages, shows the widespread involvement of Israel with music on many occasions.

Daniel 3:5, 7, 15

The use of many instruments in Babylon for the proclamation of the required worship of Nebuchadnezzar's image indicates an established pattern in the use of musical instruments. Here is one Biblical example of Gentile involvement with music.

PROJECT: Study the history of early civilizations to determine how music was intertwined with their cultures

---

5. Musicians and music teachers have had a long history in serving God.

---

1 Chronicles 6:31–33

Among the Levites listed were those whose special ministry was music. *31Now these are the men whom David appointed over the service of song in the house of the LORD, after the ark came to rest. 32They were ministering with music before the dwelling place of the tabernacle of meeting, until Solomon had built the house of the LORD in Jerusalem... 33and these are the ones who ministered with their sons: Of the sons of the Kohathites were Heman the singer....*

1 Chronicles 9:33–34

Here certain singers are mentioned who apparently lived in the immediate area and served day and night. *33These are the singers, heads of the fathers' houses of the Levites, who lodged in the chambers, and were free from other duties; for they were employed in that work day and night.*

1 Chronicles 15:16–22; 16:4–6, 41–42

David, in preparation for the bringing of the Ark to Jerusalem, directed that singers and instrumentalists should be appointed to assist in the celebration and worship. *16Then David spoke to the leaders of the Levites to appoint their brethren to be the singers accompanied by instruments of music, stringed instruments, harps, and cymbals, by raising the voice with resounding joy. 17So the Levites appointed Heman...Asaph...Ethan... 19The singers, Heman, Asaph, and Ethan, were to sound the cymbal of bronze; 20And...[eight named men] with psalteries... 21And [six others named] with harps...to excel. 22Chenaniah, leader of the Levites, was instructor in charge of the music, because he was skillful. (See also v. 27.)*

1 Chronicles 25:1–7

1Moreover David and the captains of the army separated for the service some of the sons of Asaph, of Heman, and of Jeduthun, who should prophesy with harps, stringed instruments, and cymbal.... [Verses 2–5 list the sons of these men.] 6All these were under the direction of their father for the music in the house of the LORD, with cymbals, stringed instruments, and harps, for the service of the house of God,...under the authority of the king.... 7So the number of them, with their brethren who were instructed in the songs of the LORD, all who were skillful, was two hundred and eighty-eight.

2 Chronicles 5:12–13; See also 7:6

After the building of the temple under Solomon: *12Also the Levites which were the singers...being arrayed in white linen, having cymbals, and psalteries and harps, stood at the east end of the altar, and with them an hundred and twenty priests sounding with trumpets: 13It came even to pass, as the trumpeters and singers were as one, to make one sound to be heard in praising and thanking the LORD; and when they lifted up their voice with the trumpets and cymbals and instruments of music, and praised the LORD...that then the house was filled with a cloud, even the house of the LORD.*

2 Chronicles 23:13

At the crowning of Joash king of Judah: Here were gathered trumpeters and singers with instruments, and such as taught to sing praise.

2 Chronicles 29:25–30

Under Hezekiah when temple worship was restored: Hezekiah followed the previous pattern using Levites in the house of the Lord with cymbals, psalteries, harps, priests with trumpets, singers, all in addition to congregational singing.

Ezra 2:41, 65

Israel returning from Babylon under Zerubbabel: In the detailed list of those returning are listed 128 singers, children of Asaph (v. 41), and 200 singing men and women out of the total group of 42,360 persons.

Ezra 3:9–11

Upon the completion of the foundation for the new temple in Jerusalem: *10...The priests stood in their apparel with trumpets, and the Levites, the sons of Asaph, with cymbals, to praise the LORD... 11And they sang responsively, praising and giving thanks to the LORD....*

Nehemiah 12:27–30, 42

Celebration of the completion of the wall of Jerusalem after the Captivity in Babylon: *27Now at the dedication of the wall of Jerusalem they sought out the Levites...to bring them to Jerusalem to celebrate the dedication with gladness, both with thanksgivings and singing, with cymbals and stringed instruments and harps. 28And the sons of the singers gathered together.... 29for the singers had built themselves villages all around Jerusalem.* (See also v. 46.)

Nehemiah 12:47

Supply of needs for the musicians: *In the days of Zerubbabel and in the days of Nehemiah all Israel gave the portions for the singers and the gatekeepers, a portion for each day....*

II. THE FUNCTIONS OF MUSIC

1. The major Scriptural function of music is for the praise and worship of God—a vertical function.

a. The Bible is full of examples of the use of music in worship, especially in the Old Testament.

Exodus 14:31 and 15:1–20

Singing after the crossing of the Red Sea and deliverance from Egypt.

Judges 4:23–24 and 5:1–31

Deborah and Barak singing in praise to the Lord for victory over the Canaanites.

2 Samuel 22:1–51

1Then David spoke to the LORD the words of this song, on the day when the LORD had delivered him from the hand of all his enemies, and from the hand of Saul.

1 Chronicles 15:16–28; 16:1–36, 37, 41–42

Preparing for the bringing in of the Ark to Jerusalem, David commanded the Levites to appoint musicians to lead in the rejoicing. *28Thus all Israel brought up the ark of the covenant of the LORD with shouting, and with sound of the horn, with trumpets and with cymbals, making music with stringed instruments and harps,*

1 Chronicles 25:1–7; See also 23:5

Regular use of singers and instrumentalists, under specialized leadership for the service of the house of God.

2 Chronicles 5:12–13, 7:6

Levite singers with instruments, along with 120 priests sounding trumpets, *13...were as one, to make one sound to be heard in praising and thanking the LORD...*The occasion was the placing of the Ark in the new temple which Solomon had built, and the dedication of that temple.

2 Chronicles 20:19–28

Moab invaded Judah; King Jehoshaphat led the people in a fast and prayer, asking God's help. God spoke through one of the Levites (vv. 14–17) saying that they would not need to fight, but that He would take care of the enemy. God did work, and the people and the king praised God with music both before and after the actual victory.

2 Chronicles 29:25–30; 30:21

Hezekiah and the Levites led in praise to God at the time of beginning once again the temple worship in Jerusalem after a long time of neglect and idolatry. A great Passover was kept with singing and instrumental music.

Ezra 3:10–11

When part of the Jewish people returned from captivity in Babylon and built the foundations for a new temple, there was great singing, along with a band or orchestra.

Nehemiah 12:24, 27–43

At the dedication of the rebuilt walls of Jerusalem under Nehemiah, there was great use of music. Note especially verses 24, 27, 29, 31, 35–36, 38–40. Apparently there was antiphonal music.

Matthew 26:30 and Mark 14:26

At the Last Supper, Christ and His apostles sang a hymn.

Acts 16:25

In the Philippian jail, Paul and Silas prayed and sang praises.

Revelation 15:3–4

In heaven, the redeemed will sing their praises to God: *3...Great and marvelous are Your works, Lord God Almighty! Just and true are Your ways, O King of the saints....*

b. Many biblical saints stated their personal praise to God by way of music.

Examples:

Psalm 28:7

David:...*With my song I will praise him.*

Psalm 40:3

David's testimony: *He has put a new song in my mouth—Praise to our God, Many will see it and fear, And will trust in the LORD.*

Psalm 104:33

I will sing to the LORD as long as I live, I will sing praise to my God while I have my being.

Psalm 106:12

The Psalmist recounting Israel's deliverance at the Red Sea and their songs of praise: *12Then they believed His words; They sang His praise.*

Psalm 144:9

David speaking: *I will sing a new song to You, O God; On a harp of ten strings I will sing praises to You.*

Psalm 146:2

The Psalmist says, *While I live I will praise the LORD; I will sing praises to my God while I have my being.*

Proverbs 29:6

...The righteous sings and rejoices.

Acts 2:46–47 and 4:24

In these passages, the use of music is implied.

Acts 16:25

But at midnight Paul and Silas were praying and singing hymns to God, and the prisoners were listening to them.

c. Believers of every age are encouraged to express praise in music.

Examples:

Psalm 33:2–3

2Praise the LORD with the harp: Make melody to Him with an instrument of ten strings. 3Sing to Him a new song; Play skillfully with a shout of joy.

Psalm 50:23

Whoever offers praise glorifies Me....

Psalm 68:3–4

3But let the righteous be glad; Let them rejoice before God; Yes, let them rejoice exceedingly. 4Sing to God, sing praises to His name....

Psalm 81:1–3

1Sing aloud to God our strength; Make a joyful shout to the God of Jacob. 2Raise a song and strike the timbrel, The pleasant harp with the lute. 3Blow the trumpet at the time of the New Moon, At the full moon, on our solemn feast day.

Psalm 92:1–3

1It is a good things to give thanks to the LORD, And to sing praises to Your name, O Most High: 2To declare Your lovingkindness in the morning, And Your faithfulness every night, 3On an instrument of ten strings, On the lute, And on the harp, With harmonious sound.

See also Psalms 98:1, 105:2, 135:3, 147:1; and Psalms 149–150.

Isaiah 12:5

Sing to the LORD, For He has done excellent things; this is known in all the earth. See also 42:10.

Zechariah 2:10

In the Kingdom Age: *"Sing and rejoice, O daughter of Zion; For behold, I am coming and I will dwell in your midst,"* says the LORD.

Ephesians 5:18–19

[18]Be filled with the Spirit; [19]Speaking to one another in psalms and hymns and spiritual songs, singing and making melody in your heart to the Lord.

Colossians 3:16

Let the word of Christ dwell in you richly in all wisdom; teaching and admonishing one another in psalms and hymns and spiritual songs, singing with grace in your hearts to the Lord.

Note in both of the above verses, though there is emphasis on communication to one another through music, the singing is to be done to the Lord—i.e., in worship and appreciation.

2. Music has a rightful place in the commemoration of historical events, the celebration of victories, and other special occasions.

Examples:

Exodus 15

Deliverance from Egypt and slavery; the crossing of the Red Sea.

Leviticus 25:9–10

Announcement of the year of jubilee, every fiftieth year, a year of special celebration, of setting free any bondslaves, of family reunion, a year of rest for the land.

Judges 5:1–31

Victory over the Canaanites under Deborah and Barak.

Judges 11:34

Here was a family celebration, the return of a father (Jephthah) from battle.

1 Samuel 18:6–7

David's victory over Goliath and the Philistine army.

2 Samuel 6:5, 15

The return of the Ark of the Lord to Jerusalem.

1 Kings 1:39–40

The proclamation of Solomon as the new king. *[40]And all the people went up after him; and the people played the flutes and rejoiced with great joy, so that the earth seemed to split with their sound.*

2 Chronicles 5:12–13; 7:6

The bringing in of the Ark to the temple of Solomon, and the dedication of that temple.

2 Chronicles 15:14–15

Celebration of an oath to the Lord made under King Asa, with the promise of seeking the Lord with all their hearts.

2 Chronicles 20:26–29

A triumphant victory over Moab, Ammon, and Edom, in which God miraculously killed the enemy armies in answer to the faith of Judah under Jehoshaphat.

2 Chronicles 23:12–13

The coronation of King Joash after six years of rule by the usurping Queen Athaliah.

Ezra 3:10–11

Celebration of the completion of the foundations for the new temple being built in Jerusalem by those returned from seventy years of captivity in Assyria and Babylon. (See also Neh. 12:35, 41.)

Luke 1:41–45

Elizabeth's blessing upon Mary, as she came to visit and share God's working.

Luke 1:46–56

Mary's song of rejoicing and prophecy concerning the Baby to be born to her.

Luke 1:9–14

The angel's message and praise concerning the birth of the Savior. Whether the Gloria was sung or spoken we do not know.

3. Music may express faith in God, to which He responds in giving victory.

Joshua 6

The conquest of Jericho under Joshua. See especially verses 2–20.

2 Chronicles 20:14–25

Three nations had come against Judah, invading them King Jehoshaphat was afraid, proclaimed a fast and called Judah together to seek the Lord's help (vv. 1–13). The Spirit of the Lord spoke through Jahaziel, a Levite, to the assembled congregation: *[17]"You will not need to fight in this* *battle. Position yourselves, stand still and see the salvation of the L*ORD*, who is with you, O Judah and Jerusalem!" Do not fear or be dismayed; tomorrow go out against them, for the L*ORD *is with you.* [The king, the Levites, and the people bowed before God and praised Him. The next morning the king appointed a choir.] *²²Now when they began to sing and to praise, the L*ORD *set ambushes against the people of Ammon, Moab, and Mount Seir, who had come against Judah; and they were defeated.*

"The aim and final reason of all music should be nothing else but the glory of God and the refreshment of the spirit."
—Johann Sebastian Bach (1685–1750).

---

4. Music is a method of teaching, admonishing, exhorting, and rebuking.

Deuteronomy 31:19–22; 32:1–47

God warned Moses of the coming apostasy of Israel (vv. 14–18); then He commanded Moses: *¹⁹Now therefore write down this song for yourselves, and teach it to the children of Israel; put it in their mouths, that this song may be a witness for Me against the children of Israel.... ²¹Then it shall be, when many evils and troubles have come upon them, that this song will testify against them as a witness; for it will not be forgotten in the mouths of their descendants.... ²²Moses therefore wrote this song the same day, and taught it to the children of Israel.* [The song follows in Chapter 32.]

Psalm 78 and 106

Here are remarkable examples of songs which review the history of Israel. In the preface to that history in Psalm 78 are statements which seem to indicate their purpose in teaching the next generation. *⁷⁸:²I will open now my mouth in a parable: I will utter dark sayings of old: ³Which we have heard and known, and our fathers have told us. ⁴We will not hide them from their children, Telling to the generation to come the praises of the L*ORD*, And His strength and His wonderful works that He has done. ⁵For He established a testimony in Jacob, and appointed a law in Israel, which He commanded our fathers, that they should make*

them known to their children: ⁶That the generation to come might know them, The children who would be born, That they may arise and declare them to their children. [Verses 7–8 tell the results that God desired in the next generations as a result of such teaching.]

Colossians 3:16

Here is the New Testament admonition, directing the use of songs for teaching purposes: *¹⁶Let the word of Christ dwell in you richly in all wisdom; teaching and admonishing one another in psalms and hymns and spiritual songs, singing with grace in your hearts to the Lord.*

---

5. Music is a means of communication among people—a horizontal function.

a. Music serves as a signal or alarm, or call to assembly. The trumpet and horn are especially significant for this use.

Exodus 19:13, 16, 19; 20:18

God used the sound of a trumpet, along with thunderings and lightnings to signal His giving of the Law to Moses.

Numbers 10:1–10

God gave Moses instructions for the use of two silver trumpets, which he was to make, for the sounding of calls for congregational assembly, for the gathering together of the princes, for the advancing of the various parts of the camp, for war, and for the announcement of various solemn days and offerings.

Numbers 31:6

Moses sent 1000 from each tribe to war on the Midianites, and included a trumpeter with them to sound the signals.

Judges 3:27

Ehud blew the trumpet to call together the army against the Moabites.

Judges 6:34; 7:16–22

Gideon blew the trumpet to call Abiezer and his followers together for battle against Midian; three hundred trumpets were used in God's plan for victory.

2 Samuel 2:28

Joab, David's commander, blew the trumpet and his men ended their battle with Abner and his men. (See also 18:16, 20:22.)

2 Chronicles 13:12

Abijah, king of Judah, pled with Israel under Jeroboam not to fight against Judah. Among other arguments, he said, *12...Now look, God Himself is with us as our head, and His priests with sounding trumpets to sound the alarm against you. O children of Israel, do not fight against the LORD God of your fathers, for you shall not prosper.*

Nehemiah 4:18, 20

When the people of Israel, returned from Babylon, were being harrassed by their neighbors, they carried weapons, along with their building tools. In addition, the man with the signal trumpet stayed close to Nehemiah, in case of a needed alarm.

See also Isa. 27:13; Jer. 6:1, 17; 42:14; 51:27; Ezek. 7:14, 33:3–6; Joel 2:1; Zeph. 1:16; 1 Cor. 14:8, 15:52; 1 Thes. 4:16; Heb. 12:19.

b. Music serves to refresh, to encourage, to provide enjoyment for both the performer and the listener.

Genesis 31:27

Laban reprimanded Jacob for fleeing without a musical farewell party with songs, tabrets and harp.

1 Samuel 16:15–23

When King Saul was troubled by an evil spirit, his servants said, *16Let our master now command your servants...seek out a man who is a skillful player on the harp; and it shall be that he will play it with his hand when the distressing spirit from God is upon you, and you shall be well.... 23And so it was, whenever the spirit from God was upon Saul, that David would take a harp and play it with his hand. Then Saul would become refreshed and well, and the distressing spirit would depart from him.*

2 Samuel 19:35

Barzillai had done much for David; now when Barzillai was eighty years old, David wanted to take him into the palace. Barzillai replied that, since he could no longer hear music or taste his food and drink, he would only be a nuisance to David. He therefore refused the offer. Evidently music had been a very real source of enjoyment to him in earlier years.

2 Chronicles 34:12

Music was to accompany the work of repairing the temple under King Josiah. Levites skilled with musical instruments were to be part of the crew.

Job 21:12

Job, describing the seeming happiness of the wicked, tells of their use of timbrel, harp, and organ.

Job 30:31

In speaking of his troubles, Job said, *31My harp is turned to mourning, and my flute to the voice of those who weep.* It is evident that this was not what he considered the normal use of music.

Psalm 57:7–9

David's use of music in his own devotion to the Lord: *7My heart is steadfast, O God, my heart is steadfast; I will sing and give praise. 8Awake my glory! Awake, flute and harp! I will awaken the dawn. 9I will praise You, O LORD, among the peoples; I will sing to You among the nations.*

Ecclesiastes 2:8

Solomon in his old age recounts all the things he did for enjoyment. Among other things he says, *8I also gathered for myself silver and gold and the special treasures of kings and of the provinces. I acquired male and female singers, the delights of the sons of men, and musical instruments of all kinds.*

Matthew 26:30 and Mark 14:26

At the close of Jesus' last supper with His disciples and just before His agony in the garden, He sang a hymn with them. This was a particularly trying time for all of them.

Acts 16:25

But at midnight Paul and Silas were praying and singing hymns to God, and the prisoners were listening to them. They had been imprisoned unjustly, and were in a maximum security location, with their feet in stocks, yet they found comfort and strength in song and prayer.

Ephesians 5:18–19

Characteristic of the Spirit–filled life is speaking to one another in song, singing within the heart, giving thanks always for all things.

Colossians 3:16

Our communication with one another is to include the use of songs and hymns, but we are to sing to the Lord also. Music communicates.

---

6. Music serves as an outlet for various emotions.

In addition to the many instances already cited, where music expresses praise, victory, ecstasy, and other positive emotions, here are a few samples of the use of music as an outlet for other emotions:

2 Samuel 1:17–27

Here, David laments over the death of Saul and Jonathan, and over Israel's defeat by the Philistines.

2 Chronicles 35:25 and the Book of Lamentations

25Jeremiah also lamented for Josiah [who had died]: *And to this day all the singing men and the singing women speak of Josiah in their lamentations. They made it a custom in Israel; and indeed they are written in the Laments.*

---

7. Music may be unacceptable with God because of its evil purpose or its insincerity.

Examples:

Exodus 32:18

Music and naked dancing accompanied the worship of the golden calf at Sinai.

2 Samuel 20:1–2

Sheba, a rebel from David's rule, used a trumpet to rally people to follow him and repudiate David as king.

Daniel 3:7, 15

Nebuchadnezzar used an orchestra to signal and accompany the required worship of his image. Instruments listed include *horn, flute, harp, lyre, psaltery, dulcimer, in symphony with all kinds of music.*

Amos 5:23

God is speaking to Israel, condemning their worship without any accompanying obedience: *23Take away from Me the noise of your songs, for I will not hear the melody of your stringed instruments.*

III. THE PERFORMANCE AND APPRECIATION OF MUSIC

1. Both vocal and instrumental music may be used in the worship of the Lord.

Examples:

Exodus 15:1, 20–21

Singing by the whole congregation of Israel after the crossing of the Red Sea, led by Miriam and other women with timbrels and dancing.

Judges 5:1–2

Duet by Deborah and Barak, celebrating victory for the Lord's people.

1 Samuel 10:5

A company of prophets coming from the hill of God, prophesying to the accompaniment of a psaltery, and a tabret, and a pipe, and a harp. Here is apparently unrehearsed "improvisatory" style music.

1 Chronicles 6:31–32, 9:33

Singers of the Levites had a special place in the worship connected with the tabernacle before Solomon's temple was built.

1 Chronicles 13:8; See also 15:16–24

At the bringing back of the Ark: *8Then David and all Israel played music before God with all their might, with singing, on harps, on stringed instruments, on tambourines, on cymbals, and with trumpets.* [In 15:17–24 are described several groups of singers, each with a specific kind of instrument. See also 16:4–6.]

1 Chronicles 23:5

Among the Levites were 4,000 who praised the Lord with the instruments that David made.

1 Chronicles 25:1–7

An orchestra–choir combination of 288 skilled, trained members was set up by David and his administration. Their work was to prophesy, to give thanks and praise to the Lord in the service of the house of the Lord. They were under the direction of three men (vv. 1, 6–7): Asaph, Heman, and Juduthun. They used cymbals, psalteries, and harps, and were carefully instructed in the songs of the Lord, after selection on the basis of their skill (v. 7).

2 Chronicles 5:12–13

In preparation for the dedication of the temple built under King Solomon, Levite singers, from the families of Asaph, Heman, and Juduthun stood with their cymbals, psalteries, and harps at one end of the altar, along with 120 trumpeter–priests. They sang and played together, praising the Lord.

2 Chronicles 20:21–22

After God's promise of victory over the invading armies, Jehoshaphat appointed singers to go before the army and sing God's praises.

2 Chronicles 29:25–30

Under Hezekiah, when the temple worship was restored, the king *25...Then he stationed the Levites in the house of the Lord with cymbals, with stringed instruments, and with harps...for thus was the commandment of the Lord by his prophets. 26The Levites stood with the instruments of David, and the priests with the trumpets. 27...And when the burnt offering began, the song of the Lord also began, with the trumpets and with the instruments of David king of Israel. 28So all the congregation worshiped, the singers sang, and the trumpeters sounded; all this continued until the burnt offering was finished.... 30Moreover King Hezekiah and the leaders commanded the Levites to sing praise to the Lord with the words of David and of Asaph the seer. So they sang praises with gladness, and they bowed their heads and worshiped.*

See also 2 Chronicles 30:21 and 35:15.

Ezra 2:65, 70

In the group of 42,360 Israelites and 7,337 servants who returned to Palestine under Zerubbabel, there were 200 singing men and women specifically mentioned (also mentioned in Nehemiah 7:1, 44, 73.)

Ezra 3:10–11

10When the builders laid the foundation of the temple of the Lord, the priests stood in their apparel with trumpets, and the Levites, the sons of Asaph, with cymbals, to praise the Lord, according to the ordinance of David king of Israel. 11And they sang responsively, praising and giving thanks to the Lord....

Nehemiah 10:28, 39

Among those who covenanted together to serve the Lord completely as a result of the revival under Nehemiah, singers are specifically mentioned.

Nehemiah 11:22–23

The singers were an important group: *22...Of the sons of Asaph, the singers were in charge of the service of the house of God. 23For it was the king's command concerning them that a certain portion should be for the singers, a quota day by day.*

Nehemiah 12:27–47, 13:5, 10–13

In thanks to God for the completion of the wall of Jerusalem, there was great celebration which involved a variety of instruments, singers gathered from the villages around Jerusalem, antiphonal and processional singing, participation of the women and children as well as the men. The music was directed by a leader, and those specially set apart as singers were supported by others. (See also 11:10–13.)

Psalm 68:25

The singers went before, the players on instruments followed after; among them were the damsels playing with timbrels.

See also Psalms 149–150; 1 Cor. 14:26; Eph. 5:19; Col. 3:16

---

2. A variety of musical instruments have been used in bringing praise to the Lord; some of the same instruments have also been used for evil.

---

1 Chronicles 23:5

Four thousand praised the Lord with the musical instruments, "which I made," said David, "for giving praise."

Daniel 3:5

Nebuchadnezzar's proclamation requiring

worship of his golden image: *⁵That at the time you hear the sound of the horn, flute, harp, lyre, and psaltery, in symphony with all kinds of music, you shall fall down and worship the gold image that King Nebuchadnezzar has set.*

The following brief descriptions of instruments mentioned in the Bible may be helpful. For a more complete study, consult a Bible encyclopedia, books on the history of music, or those dealing specifically with the musical instruments of the Bible. See Resource List.

Stringed Instruments

Harp: a portable stringed instrument with a sound box and usually about twelve strings to be plucked. Translated *lyre* in NASB.

Sackbut: Translated *trigon,* in NASB and *Amplified Bible,* meaning a triangular lyre, or a lute; *Berkeley* uses the term *lute;* the *New Scofield Bible* marginal note says a *stringed instrument like a lute.* In the Middle Ages, the term meant a trombone-like instrument.

Psaltery: a ten-stringed lyre, similar to a zither; a type of harp.

Sample references: Gen. 4:21; 1 Sam. 10:5; 2 Sam. 6:5; 1 Kings 10:12; 1 Chr. 15:16, 20, 28; 16:4–5; 2 Chr. 5:12; 9:10–11, 20:28, 25:1, 6, 29:25; Neh.12:27; Psa. 33:2, 43:4, 57:8–9, 71:22, 81:2, 92:1–5, 98:5, 108:2, 144:9, 147:7, 149:3, 150:3–4; Isa. 38:20; Dan. 3:5, 7, 10, 15; Hab. 3:19.

Wind Instruments

Trumpet: The term is used to indicate both the shofar, or ram's horn, and the metal horn used in the temple. This horn was a straight horn without valves, and was often used as a signal instrument.

Cornet: In several translations, the word *cornet* in KJV is translated as *horn,* with the indication that this was a smaller horn than the trumpet; however, other Bible scholars believe the cornet was actually a percussion instrument, in the form of a rattle that was shaken.

Pipe, or flute: This is believed to have been an oboe-like, double reed instrument; often two were played together. No valves, but holes to vary the pitch.

Dulcimer: Mentioned only in Daniel 3:5, 7, 10, 15, the dulcimer is believed to have been a wind

instrument like a bagpipe, and is so translated in several recent versions.

Organ: The identity of the organ is not clear. It is generally believed to be an instrument composed of several pipes, and therefore capable of producing several notes.

Sample references: 1 Sam. 10:5; 2 Sam. 6:5; 1 Kings 1:40; 1 Chr. 15:24, 28, 16:6, 42; 2 Chr. 5:12–13, 7:6, 20:28, 29:26–28; Ezra 3:10; Neh. 12:35; Psa. 81:3, 98:6, 150:3–4; Dan. 3:5, 7, 10, 15.

Percussion

Cymbals: Cymbals were of two kinds, described in Psalm 150 as loud cymbals, and high-sounding cymbals. Loud cymbals were somewhat similar to those used today, played with both hands; high-sounding cymbals were much smaller and held on the thumb and middle finger of one hand. They produced a much higher pitch.

Timbrels, or tabrets: a tambourine-like instrument, most often used by women.

Sample references to cymbals: 2 Sam. 6:5; 1 Chr. 13:8; 15:16, 19, 28; 16:5, 42; 25:1, 6; 2 Chr, 5:12–13, 29:25; Ezra 3:10; Neh. 12:27; Psa. 150:4–5.

Sample references to timbrels or tabrets: Ex. 15:20; Judges 11:34; 2 Sam. 6:5; 1 Chr. 13:8; Psa. 68:25, 81:2, 149:3, 150:3–5.

---

3. A variety of sacred music is encouraged and exemplified in the Bible.

Examples:

In the Old Testament

Psalms and songs commemorating a particular event, such as Exodus 15, Judges 5, Psalms 105:23–39, 106:7–33.

Psalms which review a long history of God's dealings, such as Psalm 78, 104, 106.

Psalms which express one persons experience and attitude toward God, such as Psalms 23 and 51.

Psalms which portray some aspect of God Himself, such as Psalm 23, 136, 139.

Psalms which exalt the Word of God, such as Psalms 19, 119.

Psalms which speak of man and his relationship to God, such as 1, 24, 42–44, 112.

Psalms which anticipate the glorious future for His people, such as Psalms 93–100.

Psalms which are pure praise and exhortation to worship, such as Psalms 146–150.

In the New Testament

Psalms, taken from the Old Testament, of various kinds.

Hymns, which express worship and commitment to the Lord.

Spiritual songs, usually considered to be songs of testimony, exhortation and instruction, for the encouragement of one another.

Significant references: Matthew 26:30; Ephesians 5:19; Colossians 3:16.

---

4. **Music and art have frequently been combined in times of worship and celebration.**

In several Scriptural incidents, the fact that the singers and/or instrumentalists wore uniforms is specifically stated.

Examples:

1 Chronicles 15:27

At the bringing back of the Ark to Jerusalem: *27David was clothed with a robe of fine linen, as were all the Levites who bore the ark, the singers, and Chenaniah the music master with the singers....*

2 Chronicles 5:12–13

Later, under Solomon, when the Ark was brought into the new temple: *12And the Levites who were the singers, all those of Asaph and Heman and Jeduthun, with their sons and their brethren, stood at the east end of the altar, clothed in white linen, having cymbals, stringed instruments and harps, and with them one hundred and twenty priests sounding with trumpets.*

Ezra 3:10–11

Many years later, after the Captivity in Babylon and the return of a remnant of Jews to their own land, the foundations of a new temple were laid. At this time, *10When the builders laid the foundation of the temple of the LORD, the priests stood in their apparel with trumpets, and the Levites, the sons of Asaph, with cymbals, to praise the LORD, according to the ordinance of David king of Israel.*

> *"It's my feeling that you can't really understand young people today unless you understand something about their music. It is in their music that young people express themselves. It's in their music that they tell you how they really feel about things."*
> —Don Wyrtzen, "What Rock Music Is Telling Our Youth," *Moody Monthly,* January, 1970.

---

5. **The beliefs, attitudes, and goals of men are reflected in the music they produce and use, or by their lack of disposition to music.**

---

a. The lack of disposition to music often indicates sadness, depression, or God's judgment.

Job 30:31

Job, in describing his troubles, says, *31My harp is turned to mourning, and my flute to the voice of those who weep.*

Psalm 137:1–4

The testimony of Jews held captive in Babylon: *1By the rivers of Babylon, there we sat down, yea, we wept, when we remembered Zion. 2We hung our harps Upon the willows in the midst of it. 3For there those who carried us away captive required of us a song, And those who plundered us required of us mirth, Saying, "Sing us one of the songs of Zion." 4How shall we sing the LORD's song in a foreign land?*

Isaiah 16:10

God's description of Moab: *10Gladness is taken away, and joy from the plentiful field; in the vineyards there will be no singing....*

Isaiah 24:8

Describing God's time of judgment: *8The mirth of the tambourine ceases, the noise of the jubilant ends, the joy of the harp ceases.*

Ezekiel 26:13

God describing the judgment of Tyre: *13I will put an end to the sound of your songs, and the sound of your harps shall be heard no more.*

Amos 8:10

God's promise of judgment to Israel: *¹⁰I will turn your feasts into mourning, and all your songs into lamentation....*

Revelation 18:22

God's description of the overthrow of the last center of rebellion against Him, here spoken of as Babylon: *²²The sound of harpists, musicians, flutists, and trumpeters shall not be heard in you anymore....*

b. The kind of music one produces, or with which he identifies, depends on his own inner thoughts and view of life.

Deuteronomy 32:17–18

Joshua and Moses, hearing the singing of the worshipers of the golden calf, sought to identify the meaning of it. In doing so, they recognized three kinds of music: shouting that indicates victory, mourning that comes with defeat, and singing that expresses delight in an activity.

Psalm 40:3

Here is the testimony of an individual, David, concerning the source of his song: *³He [the Lord] has put a new song in my mouth—Praise to our God; Many will see it and fear, And will trust in the LORD....*

Proverbs 16:9, 23

⁹A man's heart plans his way, but the LORD directs his steps.... ²³The heart of the wise teaches his mouth, and addeth learning to his lips.

Proverbs 23:7

For as he thinks in his heart, so is he....

Mark 7:20–23

²⁰And he [Jesus] said, "What comes out of a man, that defiles a man... ²¹For from within, out of the heart of men, proceed evil thoughts, adulteries, fornications, murders; ²²Thefts, covetousness, wickedness, deceit, licentiousness, an evil eye, blasphemy, pride, foolishness: ²³All these evil things come from within, and defile the man."

Luke 6:43–45

⁴³For a good tree does not bear bad fruit, nor does a bad tree bear good fruit ⁴⁴For every tree is known by its own fruit. For men do not gather figs from thorns, nor do they gather grapes from a bramble bush. ⁴⁵A good man out of the good treasure of his heart brings forth good, and an evil man out of the evil treasure of his heart brings forth evil. For out of the abundance of the heart his mouth speaks.

John 7:38–39

³⁸He who believes in Me, as the Scripture has said, out of his heart will flow rivers of living water [NKJV]. ³⁹But this spake he of the Spirit, which they that believe on him should receive.... [KJV]

Galatians 5:19–23

¹⁹Now the works of the flesh are evident, which are: adultery, fornication, uncleanness, lewdness,... ²⁰Idolatry, sorcery, hatred, contentions, jealousies, outbursts of wrath, selfish ambitions, dissensions, heresies, ²¹Envy, murders, drunkenness, revelries, and the like... ²²But the fruit of the Spirit is love, joy, peace, longsuffering, kindness, goodness, faithfulness ²³gentleness, self-control...

Ephesians 5:18–19

¹⁸Be filled with the Spirit; ¹⁹Speaking to one another in psalms and hymns and spiritual songs, singing and making melody in your heart to the Lord; ²⁰Giving thanks always for all things to God... The kinds of singing mentioned here come out of a life yielded to the Holy Spirit.

6. **Our use of music should be for the glory of God and should be tempered by its effect on others and our concern for them.**

Proverbs 25:20

Sometimes singing is inappropriate: *²⁰Like one who takes away a garment in cold weather, and like vinegar on soda, is one who sings songs to a heavy heart.*

Romans 14:15, 19, 21

The principle of concern for the feelings of others: *¹⁵Yet if your brother is grieved because of your food, you are no longer walking in love. Do not destroy with your food the one for whom Christ died.... ¹⁹Therefore let us pursue the things which make for peace and the things by which one may edify another.... ²¹It is good neither to eat meat nor drink wine nor do anything by which your brother stumbles or is offended or is made weak. (See also 1 Cor. 8:13.)*

Corinthians 6:19–20

Our bodies are to be used for God's glory. *19Or do you not know that your body is the temple of the Holy Spirit who is in you, whom you have from God, and you are not your own? 20For you were bought at a price: therefore glorify God in your body, and in your spirit, which are God's.*

Corinthians 10:23–24, 31

Some legitimate actions are not wise. *23All things are lawful for me, but all things are not helpful; all things are lawful for me, but all things do not edify. 24Let no man seek his own, but each one the other's well–being…. 31Therefore, whether you eat or drink, or whatever you do, do all to the glory of God.*

7. The sounds in music must be distinct and the words intelligible if listeners are to receive the message.

Corinthians 14:7–11

Though the primary emphasis here is on the use of the gift of speaking in other languages in an assembly of believers, the application to music is obvious. *7Even things without life, whether flute or harp, when they make a sound, unless they make a distinction in the sounds, how will it be known what is piped or played? 8For if the trumpet makes an uncertain sound, who will prepare himself for battle? 9So likewise you, unless you utter by the tongue words easy to understand, how will it be known what is spoken? For you will be speaking into the air. 10There are, it may be, languages in the world, and none of them is without signification. 11Therefore if I do not know the meaning of the language, I shall be a foreigner to him who speaks, and he who speaks will be a foreigner to me.*

8. Singers should understand what they are singing and experience the truth expressed.

1 Corinthians 14:15–16

15What is the result then? I will pray with the spirit, and I will also pray with the understanding. I will sing with the spirit, and I will also sing with the understanding.

Paul's determination.

See also Psalm 47:7; Ephesians 5:19–20; Philippians 4:8.

9. God is pleased with excellence in musical performance which is done for His glory.

1 Chronicles 15:22

After naming the lead singers in the previous verses, and indicating the instruments with which they would accompany themselves in celebration of the return of the Ark to Jerusalem, one is mentioned and the reason given for his selection: *22Chenaniah, leader of the Levites, was instructor in charge of the music, because he was skillful.*

1 Chronicles 25:7

A band of musicians was chosen, 288 in all, for a special musical ministry. They were *instructed in the songs of the Lord,* and they were cunning, or skillful with their instruments.

2 Chronicles 5:13

Indeed it came to pass, when the trumpeters and singers were as one, to make one sound to be heard in praising and thanking the Lord, and when they lifted up their voice with the trumpets and cymbals and instruments of music, and praised the Lord, saying: "For He is good, for His mercy endures forever," that the house, the house of the Lord, was filled with a cloud. Note the perfect blend and timing of the voices and instruments: they were as one, to make one sound.

10. The use of music for sinful purposes displeases God and will be judged.

Exodus 32:18–19

Music accompanying the worship of the golden calf against God's Will.

Daniel 3:5, 7, 10, 15

Music as the signal for the worship of Nebuchadnezzar's image, though God's judgment is not here specifically stated.

Isaiah 5:11–13; See also Isaiah 14:11

God describes the drunken orgies of Israel, his beloved, saying, *11Woe to those who rise early in the morning, that they may follow intoxicating drink; who continue until night, till wine inflames them!* [12]*The harp and the strings, the tambourine and flute, and wine are in their feasts; but they do not regard the work of the* LORD, *nor consider the operation of His hands.* [13]*Therefore my people have gone into captivity....*

See also II, Concept 7.

PROJECTS:

The Psalms. Use the *New American Standard Bible,* or another reliable version and note the following:

(1) Which ones are specifically labeled "For the choir director"? These were part of the choir music in David's reign. Study these psalms to see what their emphases are.

(2) Which ones note in the headings the use of specific instrumental accompaniments, or voices? You may want to consult a Bible dictionary or encyclopedia for meanings of some of the words used.

Selah. The word Selah, occurring frequently in the Psalms, may mean "Pause for meditation," or "crescendo," or a musical interlude. In any case it follows a statement or passage that warrants emphasis or further thought. Go through the Psalms, listing all the thoughts that are followed by Selah; then categorize them to determine what God wants His people to think about.

Hymn Illustration. Choose a hymn suitable for memorization by intermediate grade students, one in which the thoughts are not too abstract for illustration. Go through the hymn, line by line, thinking of types of pictures which would help to portray the truth presented, and making notes. Using old magazines and other sources, select pictures. Using a large blank book (which you may need to make by folding lightweight card stock), mount the picture and letter the words large enough for your class to see. Avoid using more than two or three double pages per stanza, or you will have difficulty turning the pages fast enough to keep up with the singing.

Health

[Fine Arts/Health]

Health:
Biblical Concepts/Background

I. GOD'S RELATIONSHIP TO OUR BODIES

1. God created man's body and is responsible for both Adam's body and ours.
2. God places high value on man's body.
   a. God considers the various parts of the body of sufficient importance to refer to many of them specifically.
   b. God uses the interrelationships among the parts of the human body as a picture of the oneness of believers in Christ, and the necessity of them all.
   c. God requires the death penalty for one who murders another person.
   d. God clearly distinguishes man from animals, both in their physical bodies and in other ways.
   e. God prepared a human body for the incarnation of His Son.
3. God cares about our needs for food, clothing, shelter, rest and exercise. He knows and cares!
   a. Our need for food
   b. Our need for clothing
   c. Our need for shelter
   d. Our need for rest
   e. Our need for exercise
4. God claims the bodies of believers as His own.
5. God expects that man will work to provide for the needs of the body. Work is part of God's plan for man.

II. THE CARE OF OUR BODIES

1. Our eating and drinking must be with awareness of God's concern.
   a. God commands moderation, warning against overeating.
   b. God forbids drunkenness, and warns against alcoholism.
   c. God gives freedom to eat all foods without defilement, though this was not true for Israel under the Law.
2. Our dress and appearance must honor God.
   a. Our bodies should be sufficiently covered that we discourage immorality.
   b. Godly women, in particular, are to be modest in their dress, hairstyle, and use of jewelry.
   c. Dress and grooming should be suitable for the occasion.
   d. Clothing need not be shabby and cheap to glorify God.
   e. Clothing should not be a source of constant worry; we should trust God for the supply of needs.
   f. We are not at liberty to mutilate our bodies.
3. Satisfying our bodies' needs for rest and sleep honors God; He warns, however, against laziness.
4. Personal cleanliness in Scripture usually represents spiritual purity in the light of God's holiness.
5. The desires of our bodies are not to be the controlling factor in our lives.
6. The body represents only one part of man; we must not overemphasize the physical, but be concerned with the whole man.

III. DISEASE AND HEALING

1. The ultimate causes of sickness and death
   a. The basic cause is the nature of man as a result of Adam's sin in the garden.
   b. Sickness and death may be the result of God's chastening upon a group of people, believers or unbelievers.
   c. Sickness and death of an individual or group may be the result of one person's sin, and God's resultant chastening.
   d. Disease and death are at times the result of the actions of parents and other ancestors. Our lifestyles affect our posterity.

e. Illness may be brought on by an attack of Satan, or by demon activity.

f. Disease may be caused, or worsened, by lack of emotional and spiritual health.

g. Physical affliction may have as its ultimate purpose the glory of God, whether or not other factors contribute.

2. Treatment and healing of disease

a. Physicians and medicines have a rightful place in healing.

b. God both prevents and heals disease, sometimes in answer to prayer, sometimes without our asking.

c. In the Apostolic Period of the history of the church, God gave the gift of healing to a limited group, as a witness to the truth of the Gospel.

d. God tells us to pray for our own healing, and for the healing of others, but He does not heal every ailment.

3. Specific diseases and deformities mentioned in the Bible

IV. MENTAL AND EMOTIONAL HEALTH

1. A variety of factors may contribute to emotional problems.

a. Poor physical health may cause emotional problems, or contribute to them.

b. Circumstances may be so overwhelming as to cause serious problems.

c. Satanic or demonic activity may be a factor in emotional problems.

d. God may judge sin by imposing a mental condition in which one is out of touch with reality.

e. Guilt over sin and failure to accept God's forgiveness may be the cause of severe depression.

f. God's refining process may necessitate our passing through some difficult places and even some low times emotionally.

2. God intends that, in general, a joyful and optimistic spirit should characterize

believers.

3. Confidence and strength depend on a proper trust in the Lord and in His promises.

4. Discerning and considerate friends are valuable assets in times of mental and emotional distress.

V. THE HANDICAPPED

1. God made man's body, even with its handicaps and limitations.

2. God sometimes has a special purpose in a handicap, which may or may not be known to the person involved.

3. God is not limited in His ability to heal or to restore, though He does not always choose to do so.

4. The Bible records many kinds of handicaps that existed in Bible times.

5. God expects us to be considerate of those with handicaps.

6. God can use people in spite of handicaps.

VI. PUBLIC HEALTH

1. Diet and foods

a. Meat should be carefully selected with particular avoidance of scavenger animals.

b. Blood should be drained from meat before it is eaten.

c. Animal fat should be avoided.

d. A safe water supply is essential to health.

2. Sanitation

a. Patients with contagious diseases should be isolated.

b. Clothing, bed linens, and utensils contaminated by disease must be thoroughly cleansed.

c. A house which, after repeated inspection and decontamination, cannot be freed from evidence of disease must be destroyed.

d. One who handles dead bodies needs cleansing before resuming his normal activities.

e. Human excrement must be disposed of in a way that will not spread contamination.

f. The discharges from seminal emission and menstruation should not be permitted to come in contact with other people.

g. Circumcision on the eighth day was prescribed by God for the descendents of Abraham and for any other boy or man born in their homes or bought with money.

3. The workweek
Six days of work plus one day of rest is God's plan for man's needs.

I. GOD'S RELATIONSHIP TO OUR BODIES

1. God created man's body and is responsible for both Adam's body and ours.

Genesis 1:27, 2:7, 21–25
The original creation: *27So God created man in His own image; in the image of God He created him; male and female He created them.... 7And the LORD God formed man of the dust of the ground, and breathed into his nostrils the breath of life; and man became a living being.... 21And the LORD God caused a deep sleep to fall on Adam, and he slept: and he took one of his ribs, and closed up the flesh in its place; 22Then the rib, which the LORD God had taken from man, He made into a woman, and brought her to the man.*

For extensive references to the creation of man in the beginning, see Book 3, or consult a topical Bible or concordance.

Psalm 139:13–16
David's personal testimony: *13For You have formed my inward parts; You have covered me in my mother's womb. 14I will praise You; for I am fearfully and wonderfully made: marvelous are Your works: and that my soul knows very well. 15My frame was not hidden from You, When I was made in secret, And skillfully wrought in the lowest parts of the earth. 16Your eyes saw my substance, being yet unformed. And in Your book they all were written, The days fashioned for me, When as yet there were none of them.*

Several facts are noteworthy: It was God who created both man and woman; He formed the man from the dust, and the woman from man, but only His breath made them living beings. Their bodies were beautiful and needed no physical covering (Genesis 1:25); they had potential to live forever (Genesis 3:22–25).

2. God places high value on man's body.

a. God considers the various parts of the body of sufficient importance to refer to many of them specifically.

Examples:
Blood: As the life in Genesis 9:5–6; Leviticus 19:16; Matthew 27:4, 24
Bones and flesh: Genesis 2:21–23; Job 19:20; Ezekiel 37:1–11
Breath: Genesis 2:7; Ezekiel 37:10; Acts 17:25
Eye and ear: Proverbs 20:12; 1 Corinthians 12:16–21
Mouth: Exodus 4:11; Psalm 19:14; Acts 3:21
Sinews: Ezekiel 37:8
Tongue: James 3:5, 8

b. God uses the interrelationships among the parts of the human body as a picture of the oneness of believers in Christ, and the necessity of them all.

Romans 12:4–5
4For as we have many members in one body, but all the members do not have the same function: 5So we, being many, are one body in Christ, and individually one members one of another.

1 Corinthians 12:12–27
Here is a more detailed explanation of the same illustration, with specific reference to a number of body parts.

See also Ephesians 4:15–16.

c. God requires the death penalty for one who murders another person.

Genesis 9:6
Before Israel and the Law: *Whoever sheds man's blood, by man his blood shall be shed; for in the image of God He made man.*

Leviticus 24:17–21

Under the Law: *¹⁷Whoever kills any man shall surely be put to death…. ¹⁹If a man causes disfigurement of his neighbor, as he has done, so shall it be done to him; ²⁰fracture for fracture, eye for eye, tooth for tooth; as he has caused disfigurement of a man, so shall it be done to him. ²¹And whoever kills an animal shall restore it; but whoever kills a man shall be put to death.*

d. God clearly distinguishes man from animals, both in their physical bodies and in other ways.

—Man was made in the image of God: Gen. 1:26, 5:1, 9:6; 1 Cor. 11:7; James 3:9.

—Man was created to have dominion over animals, not the reverse: Gen. 1:26–28; Psalm 8:6–8; Heb. 2:7–8.

—Man was able to name all the animals, but among them found no one with whom he could have fellowship, no one of his kind: Gen. 1:18, 20.

—Man had great intelligence and a large vocabulary, and the physical apparatus to enable him to speak immediately: Gen. 2:19–20.

—Man had the ability to discern and choose to obey God, while animals can only live by instinct: Gen. 1:22, 2:15–17.

—The killing of a man, under the Law, required the death penalty, while the killing of an animal belonging to another person required only the restoring of a beast for a beast. Leviticus 24:18, 21 states the distinction; the death penalty itself goes back to God's command after the Flood.

—Man has a different kind of flesh from that of animals: 1 Cor. 15:39.

—Man does not end with the death of the physical, as do animals; he lives somewhere forever: Job 19:25–27; 1 Cor. 15:20–23, 51–57; 1 Thes. 4:14–17; Heb. 9:27.

e. God prepared a human body for the incarnation of His Son.

Hebrews 2:14–18

¹⁴Inasmuch then as the children have partaken of flesh and blood, He Himself likewise shared in the same…. ¹⁶For indeed He does not give aid to angels, but He does give aid to the seed of Abraham. ¹⁷Therefore, in all things He had to be made like His brethren, that He might be a merciful and faithful High Priest in things pertaining to God….

Hebrews 10:5

Therefore, when He came into the world, He said: "Sacrifice and offering You did not desire, but a body You have prepared for Me."

Luke 2:52

The human body of our Lord grew and matured as do our bodies: *And Jesus increased in wisdom and stature, and in favor with God and men.*

3. **God cares about our needs for food, clothing, shelter, rest and exercise. He knows and cares!**

a. Our need for food

Genesis 1:29

Plants given for food in the beginning: *And God said, "See, I have given you every herb that yields seed…and every tree whose fruit yields seed; to you it shall be for food."*

Genesis 2:9

And out of the ground the Lord God made every tree grow that is pleasant to the sight and good for food…

Genesis 9:3

Meat given for food after the Flood: *Every moving thing that lives shall be food for you. I have given you all things.*

Psalm 104:14–15

¹⁴He causes the grass to grow for the cattle, And vegetation for the service of man, That he may bring forth food from the earth; ¹⁵And wine that makes glad the heart of man, Oil to make his face shine, And bread which strengthens man's heart. (See also 136:25.)

Matthew 6:25–34

²⁵"Therefore I say to you, do not worry about your life, what you will eat or what you will drink; nor about your body, what you will put on. Is not life more than food and the body more than clothing? 26Look at the birds...yet your heavenly Father feeds them. Are ye not much better than they?... 28So why do you worry about clothing? Consider the lilies of the field, how they grow: they neither toil nor spin: 29And yet I say to you that even Solomon in all his glory was not arrayed like one of these. 30Now if God so clothes the grass of the field...will He not much more clothe you, O you of little faith? 31Therefore do not worry, saying, 'What shall we eat?' or 'What shall we drink?' or 'What shall we wear?' "

1 Timothy 4:1–5

1Now the Spirit expressly says that in latter times some will depart from the faith... 3commanding to abstain from foods which God created to be received with thanksgiving by those who believe and know the truth. 4For every creature of God is good, and nothing is to be refused if it is received with thanksgiving; 5For it is sanctified by the word of God and prayer. [Though under the Law some foods were considered unclean, no longer is this true. See also Mark 7:15.]

a. Our need for clothing

Genesis 3:21

After the sin in the garden, God clothed Adam and Eve.

Deuteronomy 29:5

Moses rehearsing God's provision in the wilderness journey: *And I have led you forty years in the wilderness. Your clothes have not worn out on you, and your sandals have not worn out on your feet.* [A miraculous provision!]

Proverbs 31:21–22

In describing the virtuous woman, God comments favorably upon the clothing of her household: *21She is not afraid of snow for her household, for all her household is clothed with scarlet. 22She makes tapestry for herself; her clothing is fine linen and purple.*

Matthew 6:25, 28–32, quoted above.

Acts 9:39

God honored Dorcas by seeing that the record of her sewing to provide clothing for others is included in the Bible.

c. Our need for shelter

Scripture passages dealing with shelter are those in which God commands both Israel and New Testament believers to be concerned for hospitality, both toward their own and others.

Examples:

Leviticus 19:10, 33–34

33And if a stranger sojourns with you in your land, you shall not mistreat him. 34But the stranger who dwells among you shall be to you as one born among you, and you shall love him as yourself; for you were strangers in the land of Egypt: I am the LORD your God.

See also Exodus 23:9; Leviticus 24:22; Deuteronomy 10:18.

Matthew 25.34–46

Note especially verses 35, 40, 43, 45. This is the description of the judgment of the nations, based on their treatment of the special group of Jews who preach during the Tribulation period. (See Scofield note.) Involved is their providing shelter for God's messengers.

Romans 12:13; Hebrews 13:2; 1 Peter 4:9

Providing hospitality is described as part of the responsibility of believers.

Romans 16:1–2

Phebe is specifically commended by Paul for the hospitality she has shown to him and to others; on this basis the church at Rome is asked to receive her and assist her.

3 John 5, 8

Gaius is here commended by the Apostle John because of the many reports of his hospitality to both strangers and brethren.

1 Timothy 3:2 and Titus 1:8

One of the qualifications for pastors, or bishops, is that they are given to hospitality.

1 Timothy 5:10

One of the qualifications for widows who are to be helped by the church is that they lodged others.

d. Our need for rest

Exodus 20:9–11

9Six days shalt thou labor, and do all your work: 10But the seventh day is the Sabbath of the LORD Your God. In it you shall do no work... 11For in six days the Lord *made heavens and earth, the sea, and all that in them is, and rested the seventh day. Therefore the* Lord *blessed the Sabbath day, and hallowed it.*

1 Kings 19:4–8

When Elijah was exhausted and discouraged, the angel of the Lord came and ministered to him, giving him food and drink.

Psalm 3:5 and 4:8

David's testimony: *⁵I lay down and slept; I awoke, for the* Lord *sustained me.... ⁸I will both lie down in peace, and sleep; For You alone, O* Lord, *make me dwell in safety.*

Psalm 127:2

Sleep is God's gift to us. *It is vain for you to rise up early, to sit up late, to eat the bread of sorrows: for so He gives His beloved sleep.*

Proverbs 3:24

For one who trusts God, He says: *When you lie down, you will not be afraid; yes, you will lie down and your sleep will be sweet.*

Matthew 8:24

Jesus Himself took time to sleep even in a boat, as well as on numerous other occasions.

Mark 6:31–32

The disciples came back from their first preaching experience and excitedly told him all that had happened. He recognized their need for rest. *³¹And he said to them, "Come aside by yourselves to a deserted place and rest a while." For there were many coming and going, and they did not even have time to eat. ³²So they departed to a deserted place in the boat by themselves.*

e.   Our need for exercise

Proverbs 31:17

The virtuous woman is described: *She girds herself with strength, and strengthens her arms.*

Ecclesiastes 5:12

*The sleep of a laboring man is sweet, whether he eats little or much:...*In other words, exercise promotes sound sleep.

1 Timothy 4:8

For bodily exercise profits a little [or for a little].

See also passages in the later chapter entitled "Physical Education and Athletics," for references to athletic competition.

4. God claims the bodies of believers as His own.

Romans 12:1

I beseech you therefore, brethren, by the mercies of God, that you present your bodies a living sacrifice, holy, acceptable to God, which is your reasonable service.

1 Corinthians 6:13, 15

¹³Now the body is not for sexual immorality but for the Lord, and the Lord for the body. ¹⁵Do you not know that your bodies are members of Christ?

1 Corinthians 6:19–20

¹⁹Or do you not know that your body is the temple of the Holy Spirit who is in you, whom you have from God, and you are not your own? ²⁰For you were bought at a price; therefore glorify God in your body and in your spirit, which are God's.

2 Corinthians 6:16

And what agreement has the temple of God with idols? For you are the temple of the living God. As God has said: "I will dwell in them and walk among them. I will be their God, and they shall be My people."

1 Thessalonians 5:23

Now may the God of peace Himself sanctify you [or set you apart] *completely; and may your whole spirit, soul, and body be preserved blameless at the coming of our Lord Jesus Christ.*

2 Timothy 2:21

Therefore if anyone cleanses himself from the latter, he will be a vessel for honor, sanctified and useful for the Master, prepared for every good work.

5. God expects that man will work to provide for the needs of the body. Work is part of God's plan for man.

Proverbs 28:19

He who tills his land will have plenty of bread, but he who follows frivolity will have poverty enough.

Proverbs 31:10–31

God's description of a virtuous woman includes several statements that indicate her industriousness in order to feed and clothe her family, as well as help others in need. *²⁷She watches over the ways of her household, and does not eat the bread of idleness.*

2 Thessalonians 3:8, 10–12

Paul's testimony and then his exhortation to the saints: *⁸Nor did we eat anyone's bread free of charge, but worked with labor and toil night and day, that we might not be a burden to any of you.... ¹⁰For even when we were with you, we commanded you this: If anyone will not work, neither shall he eat. ¹¹For we hear that there are some who walk among you in a disorderly manner, not working at all, but are busybodies. ¹²Now those who are such we command and exhort through our Lord Jesus Christ that they work in quietness and eat their own bread.*

II. THE CARE OF OUR BODIES

1. Our eating and drinking must be with awareness of God's concern.

a. God commands moderation, warning against overeating.

Proverbs 23:1–3, 20–21

¹When you sit down to eat with a ruler, Consider carefully what is before you: ²And put a knife to your throat if you are a man given to appetite. ³Do not desire his delicacies, for they are deceptive food. ²⁰Do not mix with winebibbers, or with gluttonous eaters of meat: ²¹For the drunkard and the glutton will come to poverty, and drowsiness will clothe a man with rags.

Daniel 1:3–21

An excellent example of young men who refused to indulge in the rich food and drink of the foreign palace and thereby proved the superiority of plainer foods.

Matthew 15:32–38

Jesus recognizes the necessity of food if people are not to faint along the way; as a result He feeds the multitude: *³²Then Jesus called His*

disciples to Him, and said, "I have compassion on the multitude, because they have now continued with Me three days and have nothing to eat. And I do not want to send them away hungry, lest they faint on the way."* [Food is necessary for the body! Too long a fast is dangerous, too.]

Acts 27:33–36

Here, too, is recognition on Paul's part of the necessity of eating if the sailors were to be able to survive the storm. *³³Paul implored them all to take food, saying, "Today is the fourteenth day you have waited and continued without food, and eaten nothing. ³⁴Therefore I urge you to take nourishment, for this is for your survival, since not a hair will fall from the head of any of you." ³⁵And when he had said these things, he took bread and gave thanks to God in the presence of them all; and when he had broken it he began to eat. ³⁶Then they were all encouraged, and also took food themselves.*

1 Corinthians 9:25

And everyone who competes for the prize is temperate in all things. Now they do it to obtain a perishable crown, but we for an imperishable crown.

1 Corinthians 10:31

Therefore, whether you eat or drink, or whatever you do, do all to the glory of God.

Titus 1:12–13

Paul, in encouraging Titus about how a church should function, calls to his attention the fact that in his church on the Island of Crete, some were slow bellies, or lazy gluttons. He further directs Titus that he should rebuke them sharply.

b. God forbids drunkenness, and warns against alcoholism.

Deuteronomy 21:18–21

Here, in the Law for Israel, God associates stubbornness, rebelliousness, refusal to submit to parents, gluttony, and drunkenness, and then says that such a person is to be stoned in order to keep the nation from sin.

Proverbs 20:1

Wine is a mocker, strong drink is raging: and whosoever is deceived thereby is not wise.

Proverbs 23:20–21, 29–35

²⁰Do not mix with winebibbers [heavy drinkers]; *²¹for the drunkard and the glutton will come to poverty, and drowsiness will clothe a man with rags.... ²⁹Who has woe? Who has sorrow? Who has contentions? Who has complaints? Who has wounds without cause? Who has redness of eyes? ³⁰Those who linger long at the wine, those who go in search of mixed wine. ³¹Do not look on the wine when it is red.... ³²At the last it bites like a serpent, and stings like a viper. ³³Your eyes will see strange things, and your heart will utter perverse things.* [Note all the effects of drunkenness: poverty, woe, sorrow, quarreling, meaningless babbling, wounds, bleary eyes, relationships with strange women, etc.]

Proverbs 31:4–5

Drunkenness is particularly improper for those in authority, since they have great responsibilities and need all their faculties: *⁴It is not for kings, O Lemuel, it is not for kings to drink wine; nor for princes intoxicating drink: ⁵Lest they drink, and forget the law, and pervert the justice of all the afflicted.*

Isaiah 5:11, 22

¹¹Woe to those who rise early in the morning, that they may follow intoxicating drink; who continue until night, till wine inflames them.... ²²Woe to men mighty at drinking wine, woe to men valiant for mixing intoxicating drink.

Isaiah 28:1, 3, 7–8

God condemns the drunkards of Ephraim: *¹Woe to the crown of pride, to the drunkards of Ephraim, whose glorious beauty is a fading flower.... ³The crown of pride, the drunkards of Ephraim, will be trampled underfoot;... ⁷But they also have erred through wine, and through intoxicating drink are out of the way; the priest and the prophet have erred through intoxicating drink, they are swallowed up by wine, they are out of the way through intoxicating drink; they err in vision, they stumble in judgment.*

Luke 21:34

But take heed to yourselves, lest your hearts be weighed down with carousing, drunkenness, and cares of this life, and that Day [i.e., the day of the Lord's return] *come on you unexpectedly.*

Romans 13:13

Let us walk properly, as in the day, not in revelry and drunkenness, not in licentiousness and lewdness [NASB: *not in sexual promiscuity and sensuality*] *not in strife and envying.*

Galatians 5:19–21

¹⁹Now the works of the flesh are evident, which are:... ²¹drunkenness, revellings, and the like: of the which I tell you...that those who practice such things will not inherit the kingdom of God.

Ephesians 5:18

And do not be drunk with wine, in which is dissipation; but be filled with the Spirit. God's desire is that we be under the control of the Spirit, rather than under the control of wine.

1 Timothy 3:2–3, 8

²A bishop [or pastor] *then must be... ³Not given to wine... ⁸Likewise deacons must be reverent, not double-tongued, not given to much wine....*

> "Look to your health; and if you have it, praise God and value it next to a good conscience; for health is the second blessing that we mortals are capable of—a blessing that money cannot buy; therefore value it, and be thankful for it."
> —Izaak Walton (1593–1683), English author.

c. God gives freedom to eat all foods without defilement, though this was not true for Israel under the Law.

Matthew 15:11

Not what goes into the mouth defiles a man; but what comes out of the mouth, this defiles a man. [Here, He was saying that eating food with unwashed hands does not defile a man. See also Mark 7:15.]

1 Corinthians 8:4, 8

Here, the reference is to meat that has been previously offered to idols. *⁴Therefore concerning the eating of things offered to idols, we know that an idol is nothing in the world, and that there is no other God but one.... ⁸But food does not commend us to God; for neither if we eat are we the better, nor if we do not eat are we the worse.*

Colossians 2:16–17

16Therefore let no one judge you in food or in drink, or regarding a festival or a new moon or sabbaths: 17Which are a shadow of things to come; but the substance is of Christ.

1 Timothy 4:1–5

1Now the Spirit expressly says that in latter times some will depart from the faith... 3commanding to abstain from foods which God created to be received with thanksgiving by those who believe and know the truth. 4For every creature of God is good, and nothing is to be refused if it is received with thanksgiving.

---

2. **Our dress and appearance must honor God.**

---

a. Our bodies should be sufficiently covered that we discourage immorality.

Genesis 3:7, 10, 21

As soon as Adam and Eve sinned, they knew that they were naked and should be covered; they made fig leaf garments; God made coats of skin.

Genesis 9:21–27

Noah lay drunk in his tent. His son, Ham, saw his naked body; Shem and Japheth covered him without seeing his body. Noah awakened and knew what had happened and pronounced a curse upon Canaan, Ham's son, because of Ham's seeing his father's drunken, naked body. Nakedness was recognized as improper.

Exodus 20:26

In giving of the Law, God gave some specific instructions concerning the building of altars in order to prevent exposure of the body of a worshiper: *26Nor shall you go up by steps to My altar, that your nakedness may not be exposed on it.*

Exodus 32:25

Nakedness was associated with idol worship. At the time of the golden calf: *Now when Moses saw that the people were unrestrained (for Aaron had not restrained them, to their shame among their enemies)...*

2 Samuel 11:2–4

After seeing Bathsheba's nakedness during her bath, David became involved in adultery: *2Then it happened one evening that David arose from his bed and walked on the roof of the king's house. And from the roof he saw a woman bathing, and the woman was very beautiful to behold. 3So David sent and inquired about the woman.... 4Then David sent messengers, and took her; and she came to him, and he lay with her....*

Luke 8:27, 35

When the man of Gadara was possessed with demons, he wore no clothes and lived in the tombs. After Jesus cast out the demons, he was found *sitting at the feet of Jesus, clothed, and in his right mind.*

1 Thessalonians 5:22

Abstain from every form of evil.

b. Godly women, in particular, are to be modest in their dress, hairstyle, and use of jewelry.

1 Timothy 2:9–10

9In like manner also, that the women adorn themselves in modest apparel, with propriety and moderation, not with braided hair or gold or pearls or costly clothing; 10But which is proper for women professing godliness, with good works.

1 Peter 3:1–5

1Likewise, you wives... 3Do not let your beauty be that outward adorning of arranging the hair, of wearing gold, or of putting on fine apparel; 4But let it be the hidden person of the heart, with the incorruptible ornament of a gentle and quiet spirit, which is very precious in the sight of God. 5For in this manner, in former times, the holy women who trusted in God also adorned themselves, being submissive to their own husbands.

c. Dress and grooming should be suitable for the occasion.

Examples:

Genesis 41:14

Then Pharaoh sent and called Joseph, and they brought him hastily out of the dungeon: and he shaved, changed his clothing, and came to

H E A L T H

Pharaoh. [Even in a time of crisis, he took time.]

Esther 2:12–13, 5:1

The candidates for queen in Shushan were prepared for twelve months under the care of a special official. Then when it was a girl's turn to go in to the king: *¹³Thus prepared, each young woman went to the king, and she was given whatever she desired to take with her from the women's quarters to the king's palace.* Esther asked nothing extra when her turn came. However, later, when she appeared before the king in an effort to save her people, she put on her royal apparel.

d. Clothing need not be shabby and cheap to glorify God.

Proverbs 31:21–22

The virtuous woman is here described as dressing well, herself as well as her family. *²¹She is not afraid of snow for her household: for all her household is clothed with scarlet. ²²She makes tapestry for herself; her clothing is fine linen and purple.*

e. Clothing should not be a source of constant worry; we should trust God for the supply of needs.

Matthew 6:25–34

²⁵"Do not worry...about your body, what you will put on. Is not life more than food and the body more than clothing?... ²⁸So why do you worry about clothing? Consider the lilies of the field, how they grow: they neither toil nor spin: ²⁹And yet I say to you, That even Solomon in all his glory was not arrayed like one of these. ³⁰Now if God so clothes the grass of the field, which today is, and tomorrow is thrown into the oven, will He not much more clothe you, O you of little faith? ³¹Therefore do not worry, saying, 'What shall we eat?' or 'What shall we drink?' or 'What shall we wear?' ³²For after all these things the Gentiles seek. For your heavenly Father knows that you need all these things. ³³But seek first the kingdom of God and His righteousness, and all these things shall be added to you."

f. We are not at liberty to mutilate our bodies.

Leviticus 19:28

You shall not make any cuttings in your flesh for the dead, nor tattoo any marks on you: I am the Lord.

Deuteronomy 14:1–2

¹You are the children of the Lord your God: you shall not cut yourselves nor shave the front of your head for the dead. ²For you are a holy people to the Lord your God, and the Lord has chosen you to be a people for Himself a special treasure above all the peoples who are on the face of the earth.

Note: Though these two passages refer primarily to Israel, their application to believers today is in keeping with what God says about our bodies being God's temples.

3. **Satisfying our bodies' needs for rest and sleep honors God; He warns, however, against laziness.**

Genesis 18:4

Here the three men who were messengers from God to Abraham agreed to Abraham's suggestion that they rest and eat, even before they presented their message concerning the birth of Isaac.

Exodus 35:2–3

Here was rest on the sabbath day to be enforced by law. The Sabbath was to be *a day of rest to the Lord.*

Psalm 23:2–3

²He makes me to lie down in green pastures; He leads me beside the still waters. ³He restores my soul.... (See also David's testimony to God's protection while he slept: Psalm 3:5 and 4:8).

Psalm 127:2

God says it is impossible to get up too early and sit up too late, involved with our problems: *²It is vain for you to rise up early, to sit up late, to eat the bread of sorrows: for so he gives His beloved sleep.*

Proverbs 6:9–11

⁹How long will you slumber, O sluggard? When will you rise from your sleep? ¹⁰A little sleep, a little slumber, a little folding of the hands to sleep: ¹¹So shall your poverty come on you like a robber, and your need like an armed man. (See also 24:33–34.)

49

Proverbs 10:5

He who gathers in summer is a wise son, but he who sleeps in harvest is a son who causes shame.

Proverbs 19:15

Slothfulness casts one into a deep sleep, and an idle person will suffer hunger.

Ecclesiastes 5:12

The sleep of a laboring man is sweet, whether he eats little or much: but the abundance of the rich will not permit him to sleep.

---

4. Personal cleanliness in Scripture usually represents spiritual purity in the light of God's holiness.

Exodus 19:10–11

Before the giving of the Law to Moses and to Israel, they were to set themselves apart and wash their clothes: *[10]Then the LORD said to Moses, "Go to the people and sanctify them today and tomorrow, and let them wash their clothes, [11]And let them be ready for the third day. For on the third day the LORD will come down upon Mount Sinai in the sight of all the people."*

Leviticus 14:8–10

Before the cleansed leper could make his sacrifice to the Lord and be pronounced clean: *[8]He who is to be cleansed shall wash his clothes, shave off all his hair, and wash himself in water, that he may be clean:... [9]But on the seventh day... wash his clothes, and wash his body in water, and he shall be clean. [10]And on the eighth day he shall take two male lambs....*

Leviticus 15:13–14

Similarly one who had a hemorrhage and was cured was required to wash his body and his clothes and wait seven days before bringing his offering to the Lord.

Numbers 8:21–22

The Levites, too, must cleanse themselves before serving the Lord: *[21]And the Levites were purified themselves and washed their clothes; then Aaron presented them, as though a wave offering before the LORD, and Aaron made atonement for them to cleanse them. [22]After that the Levites went in to do their work in the tabernacle....*

Numbers 19:7–8, 10, 19, 21

In the offering of the red heifer, the priest, as well as the one who burned the body, and the man who gathered the ashes of the dead animal— all were to wash both clothes and bodies in order to be clean before the Lord.

Psalm 51:2, 7

David's prayer: *Wash me thoroughly from my iniquity, And cleanse me from my sin. [7]Purge me with hyssop, and I shall be clean: Wash me, and I shall be whiter than snow.*

Matthew 15:2–11

Here, Jesus explains that it is not eating with unwashed hands that defiles a man, but rather he is defiled by what he says. (See also Mark 7:2–9.)

Luke 11:38–39

[38]And when the Pharisee saw it, he marveled that He had not first washed before dinner. [39]But the Lord said to him, "Now you Pharisees make the outside of the cup and dish clean, but your inward part is full of greed and wickedness." (See also Matthew 23:25–29.)

John 13:2–17

Here, Jesus washes the feet of the disciples. Without doubt there was the need of the physical cleansing, but he used the incident primarily to give them an illustration of humility.

"Evil into the mind of God or man, may come and go, and yet, if unapproved, still without sin."
—John Milton (1608–1674), English poet.

---

5. The desires of our bodies are not to be the controlling factor in our lives.

Matthew 18:6

Even physical life itself is not as important as obeying God: *[6]But whoever causes one of these little ones who believe in Me to sin, it would be better for him if a millstone were hung around his neck, and he were drowned in the depth of the sea.*

Matthew 18:8–9

It is better to be physically handicapped than to suffer everlasting punishment in hell: *[8]And if your hand or foot causes you to sin, cut it off and cast it from you. It is better for you to enter into life lame or maimed, rather than having two hands or two feet, to be cast into the everlasting fire. ⁹And if your eye causes you to sin [NASB: causes thee to stumble], Pluck it out, and cast it from you. It is better for you to enter into life with one eye, rather than having two eyes, to be cast into hell fire.*

Romans 8:12–13

¹²Therefore, brethren, we are debtors, not to the flesh, to live according to the flesh. ¹³For if you live according to the flesh you will die; but if by the Spirit you put to death the deeds of the body, you will live.

1 Corinthians 6:12–20

¹²All things are lawful unto me, but all things are not expedient; all things are lawful for me, but I will not be brought under the power of any.

1 Corinthians 9:25–27

²⁵And everyone who competes for the prize is temperate in all things. Now they do it to obtain a perishable crown, but we for an imperishable crown. ²⁶Therefore I run thus: not with uncertainty. Thus I fight: not as one who beats the air: ²⁷But I discipline my body and bring it into subjection, lest, when I have preached to others, I myself should become disqualified.

Galatians 5:24

And those who are Christ's have crucified the flesh with its passions and desires.

1 Thessalonians 4:3–5

³For this is the will of God, your sanctification: that you should abstain from sexual immorality: ⁴That each of you should know how to possess his own vessel in sanctification and honor; ⁵Not in passion of lust, like the Gentiles who do not know God.

---

6. The body represents only one part of man; we must not overemphasize the physical, but be concerned with the whole man.

Genesis 1:26–27, 2:7

²⁶Then God said, "Let Us make man in Our image, according to Our likeness; let them have dominion...." ²⁷So God created man in His own image, in the image of God He created him; male

and female He created them. ⁷And the LORD God formed man of the dust of the ground, and breathed into his nostrils the breath of life; and man became a living being. (See also Isaiah 43:7.)

2 Kings 7:1–11

Here is the account of four lepers who, in spite of leprosy, visited the enemy camp, found it deserted, and spread the news. Their physical handicap did not make them useless.

Proverbs 11:22

As a ring of gold in a swine's snout, so is a lovely woman who lacks discretion. [Beauty of figure does not count for much without other characteristics.]

Ecclesiastes 6:2–3

²A man to whom God has given riches and wealth and honor, so that he lacks nothing for himself of all he desires; yet God does not give him power to eat of it, but a foreigner consumes it. This is vanity, and it is an evil affliction. ³If a man begets a hundred children, and lives many years, so that the days of his years are many, but his soul is not satisfied with goodness,...I say that a stillborn child is better than he. [In other words, plenty is of little value without health to enjoy it, but long life and old age without good character is also of little value.]

Matthew 5:29–30, and Mark 9:43–48

Jesus warns that the loss of an eye, or hand or foot is to be preferred to everlasting punishment in hell.

Matthew 6:25–26

²⁵Therefore I say to you, do not worry about your life, what you will eat or what you will drink; nor about your body, what you will put on. Is not life more than food and the body more than clothing? ²⁶Look at the birds...yet your heavenly Father feeds them. Are you not of more value than they?

Matthew 10:28

And do not fear those who kill the body but cannot kill the soul. But rather fear Him who destroy both soul and body in hell.

Matthew 16:26

For what is a man profited, if he gains the whole world and loses his own soul? Or what will a man give in exchange for his soul?

Luke 2:40, 52

In His incarnation, the Son of God took on Him a human body, but the body was not all: *⁴⁰And the Child grew and became strong in spirit, filled with wisdom; and the grace of God was upon Him.... ⁵²And Jesus increased in wisdom and stature, and in favor with God and man.*

1 Thessalonians 5:23

Now may the God of peace Himself sanctify [or, set apart] you completely; and may your whole spirit, soul, and body be preserved blameless at the coming of our Lord Jesus Christ.

1 Timothy 4:7–8

⁷But refuse profane and old wives' fables, and exercise yourself rather to godliness. ⁸For bodily exercise profits a little, but godliness is profitable for all things, having promise of the life that now is, and of that which is to come.

III. DISEASE AND HEALING

1. The ultimate causes of sickness and death

a. The basic cause is the nature of man as a result of Adam's sin in the garden.

Genesis 2:17

But of the tree of the knowledge of good and evil you shall not eat, for in the day that you eat of it you shall surely die. [God's promises when He placed man in the garden.]

Job 5:6–7

Eliphaz speaking to Job: *⁶For affliction does not come from the dust, nor does trouble spring from the ground; ⁷Yet man is born to trouble, as the sparks fly upward.*

Romans 5:12

Therefore, just as through one man sin entered the world, and death through sin, and thus death spread to all men, because all sinned.

1 Corinthians 15:21–22

²¹For since by man came death, by Man also came the resurrection of the dead. ²²For as in Adam all die, even so in Christ all shall be made alive.

b. Sickness and death may be the result of God's chastening upon a group of people, believers or unbelievers.

Exodus 15:26

God speaking to Israel after their release from Egypt: *²⁶If you diligently heed the voice of the Lᴏʀᴅ your God and do what is right in His sight, give ear to His commandments and keep all His statutes, I will put none of the diseases on you which I have brought on the Egyptians. For I am the Lᴏʀᴅ who heals you.* (See also 23:25, 30:12.)

Leviticus 26:14–16, 21, 25

¹⁴But if you do not obey Me ... ¹⁵And if you despise My statutes ... ¹⁶terror over you, wasting disease and fever which shall consume the eyes and cause sorrow of heart ... ²¹plagues, according to your sins ... ²⁵pestilence....

Numbers 11:33–34

When Israel complained about the food, God sent quails, more than they could eat, but He also smote the people with a very great plague. *³⁴So he called the name of that place Kibroth Hattaavah, because there they buried the people who had yielded to craving.*

Numbers 14:36–37

When the spies returned from the promised land and the ten men made all the congregation to murmur against the Lord, *³⁷Those very men who brought the evil report about the land, died by the plague before the Lᴏʀᴅ.*

Numbers 16:28–32, 35, 49–50

When Korah led 250 men in a rebellion against Moses, whom God had appointed, God caused the earth to swallow up Korah; He sent fire to consume the 250 men who offered incense out of turn; and He sent a plague which struck and killed 14,700 others.

Deuteronomy 7:12–15

God promised Israel that in return for obedience, He would bless them. Among other promises was this: *¹⁵And the Lᴏʀᴅ will take away from you all sickness, and will afflict you with none of the terrible diseases of Egypt which you have known, but will lay them on all those who hate you.* (See also 28:21–22, 27, 29, 35.)

1 Samuel 5:6

When the Philistines captured the ark of God, it became a curse to them: *⁶But the hand of the LORD was heavy on the people of Ashdod, and He ravaged them and struck them with tumors, both Ashdod and its territory.*

Revelation 22:18

God does not limit His use of sickness and death as judgment to the period of the Law, for He says here: *¹⁸For I testify to everyone who hears the words of the prophecy of this book: if anyone adds to these things, God will add to him the plagues that are written in this book.*

c. Sickness and death of an individual or group may be the result of one person's sin, and God's resultant chastening.

Numbers 12:9–15

Aaron and Miriam complained against the leadership of Moses; God smote Miriam with leprosy (vv. 9–10).

2 Samuel 24:10, 15, 17

Because David as king sinned in ordering a census of the people against God's will, 70,000 men died by God's sending a pestilence.

1 Kings 13:4

A man of God remonstrated with Jeroboam about the altar he had wrongly built in Bethel. Jeroboam angrily put his hand on the altar and attempted to restrain the man of God. Immediately his hand dried up and he could not withdraw it.

2 Kings 5:20–27

When Gehazi, Elisha's servant greedily sought the reward which his master had refused, Elisha said to him: *²⁷"Therefore the leprosy of Naaman shall cling to you and your descendants forever." And he went out from his presence leprous, as white as snow.*

2 Chronicles 21:14–15, 18–19

Because King Jehoram of Judah turned away from God, God sent Elijah with a message of judgment involving sickness and, after two years, death: *¹⁴Behold, the LORD will strike your people with a serious affliction—your children, your wives, and all your possessions: ¹⁵And you will become very sick with a disease of your intestines, until your*
intestines, come out by reason of the sickness, day by day.... *¹⁸After all this the LORD struck him in his intestines with an incurable disease. ¹⁹Then it happened in the course of time, after the end of two years, that his intestines came out because of his sickness; so he died in severe pain.*

2 Chronicles 26:16–21

King Uzziah of Judah became proud and dared to go into the temple of the Lord to burn incense, an act that belonged only to the priest. When the priest rebuked him, he became angry. *²⁰And Azariah the chief priest, and all the priests, looked upon him, at him, and there, on his forehead, he was leprous; so they thrust him out of that place. Indeed he also hurried to get out, because the LORD had struck him.*

Acts 5:5–6, 10

Ananias and Sapphira were judged by God for lying about what they had given to the Lord.

1 Corinthians 11:29–30

Paul warns about careless partaking of the Lord's Supper, saying that the result in some cases is sickness and even death. *²⁹For he who eats and drinks in an unworthy manner eats and drinks judgment to himself, not discerning the Lord's body. ³⁰For this reason many are weak and sick among you, and many sleep.*

It is apparent that though more cases of sickness and death as judgment from God are described in the Old Testament, the possibility exists also for believers today.

d. Disease and death are at times the result of the actions of parents and other ancestors. Our lifestyles affect our posterity.

Exodus 12:29

When the leaders of Egypt refused to let Israel go, *²⁹... The LORD struck all the firstborn in the land of Egypt, from the firstborn of Pharaoh who sat on his throne to the firstborn of the captive who was in the dungeon....*

Exodus 20:5–6

⁵Thou shall not bow down to them [i.e., graven images], nor serve them. For I, the LORD your God, am a jealous God, visiting the iniquity of the fathers on the children to the third and fourth generations of those who hate Me; ⁶But showing mercy to thousands, to those who love Me and keep My commandments. (See also 34:7; Numbers 14:18; Jeremiah 32:18.)

Numbers 16:32

When Korah rebelled, his family and the families of his followers suffered as well as he did.

Deuteronomy 28:32, 41, 53–62

God, in stating the results of Israel's failure to obey Him, predicted: *32Your sons and your daughters shall be given to another people, and your eyes shall look and fail with longing for them all day long; and there shall be no strength in your hand.... 41You shall beget sons and daughters, but they shall not be Yours; for they shall go into captivity.* [vv. 53–66 speak of the cannibalism and disease which would be rampant in that day.]

Joshua 7:24–25

Likewise, when Achan sinned, his sons, daughters, and all his animals were stoned for his sin.

1 Kings 21:29

Ahab had been a wicked king in Israel. Toward the end of his life he repented before God. The result was that God promised not to bring evil in his days, but instead in the days of his son.

Daniel 6:24

After God had preserved Daniel in the lion's den, the king commanded that the men who accused Daniel, together with their wives and children be cast into the den.

e. Illness may be brought on by an attack of Satan, or by demon activity.

Job 1:6–12 and 2:3–7

Satan, with God's permission, attacked Job's property, his family, and his body, covering him with boils from head to foot.

Matthew 8:28–34 and Mark 5:2–20

The man of Gadara who lived in the tombs as possessed with demons; as a result he was mentally deranged. Note Mark 5:4–5, 15 especially.

Matthew 9:32–33

When the demon was cast out of the dumb man, he was able to speak. Evidently the demon was the cause of the physical disability. So also in

Matthew 12:22, where the casting out of a demon enabled the blind and dumb man to see and speak again. (See also Luke 11:14.)

Mark 9:17–27 and Luke 9:38–43

A demon repeatedly caused a boy to have seizures of some kind. The physical symptoms included foaming at the mouth, gnashing his teeth, tearing his flesh, pining away. This had gone on since childhood. Jesus cast out the demon in response to the faith of the boy's father.

Luke 13:11–12, 16

11And, behold, there was a woman who had a spirit of infirmity eighteen years, and was bent over and could in no way raise herself up. 12But when Jesus saw her, He called her to Him and said to her, "Woman, you are loosed from your infirmity...." 16So ought not this woman, being a daughter of Abraham, whom Satan has bound—think of it—for eighteen years, be loosed from this bond on the Sabbath?

2 Corinthians 12:7

Paul speaks here of his *thorn in the flesh, the messenger of Satan.*

f. Disease may be caused, or worsened, by lack of emotional and spiritual health.

Job 5:2

For wrath kills a foolish man, and envy slays a simple one.

Psalm 38:3

There is no soundness in my flesh because of Your anger: Nor is there any health in my bones Because of my sin.

Psalm 102:3–11

3For my days are consumed like smoke, And my bones are burned like a hearth. 4My heart is stricken and withered like grass, So that I forget to eat my bread. 5Because of the sound of my groaning My bones cling to my skin.... 8My enemies reproach me all day long, And those who deride me swear an oath against me. 9For I have eaten ashes like bread, and mingled my drink with weeping, 10Because of Your indignation and Your wrath; For You have lifted me up and cast me away. 11My days are like a shadow that lengthens, And I wither away like grass. [Here because of affliction is loss of weight, no appetite, broken health, depression, rapid aging.]

Proverbs 11:19

As righteousness leads to life, so he who pursues evil pursues it to his own death.

Proverbs 14:30

A sound heart is life to the body, but envy is rottenness to the bones.

Proverbs 16:24

Pleasant words are like a honeycomb, sweetness to the soul and health to the bones.

g. Physical affliction may have as its ultimate purpose the glory of God, whether or not other factors contribute.

2 Kings 6:18–20

The Syrians were attacking Israel. Elisha prayed that God would smite them with temporary blindness, so they could be led away into Samaria. The result: *The hands of Syria came no more into the land of Israel* (v. 23).

Job 42:5–6, 10, 12

After all his trials, Job said, *⁵I have heard of You by the hearing of the ear, but now my eye sees You. ⁶Therefore I abhor myself, and repent in dust and ashes.... ¹⁰And the LORD restored Job's losses when he prayed for his friends. Indeed the LORD gave Job twice as much as he had before.... ¹²Now the LORD blessed the latter days of Job more than his beginning....*

Psalm 119:67–68

The Psalmist's testimony: *⁶⁷Before I was afflicted I went astray: but now have I keep your word. ⁶⁸You are good, and do good; Teach me Your statutes.*

Proverbs 3:12

For whom the LORD loves He corrects, just as a father the son in whom he delights.

Proverbs 17:22

A merry heart does good, like medicine, but a broken spirit dries the bones.

Proverbs 18:14

The spirit of a man will sustain him in sickness, but who can bear a broken spirit?

Isaiah 40:28–31

²⁸God, the LORD, the Creator of the ends of the earth, neither faints nor is weary.... ²⁹He gives power to the weak, and to those who have no might He increases strength. ³⁰Even the youths shall faint and be weary, and the young men shall utterly fall; ³¹But those who wait on the LORD shall renew their strength; they shall mount up with wings like eagles, they shall run and not be weary, they shall walk and not faint.

Hosea 4:10–11

God describes Israel in sin; among other things He says: *¹⁰For they shall eat, but not have enough; they shall commit harlotry, but not increase; because they have ceased obeying the LORD. ¹¹Harlotry, wine, and new wine enslave the heart.* [Failure to assimilate food and bear children.]

Luke 13:1–5

Here, the Lord cites two instances when the tragedy that happened to groups of people was not caused by their sin: *²Do you suppose that these Galileans were worse sinners than all other Galileans, because they suffered such thing? ³I tell you, No,... ⁴Or those eighteen, on whom the tower in Siloam fell and killed them, do you think that they were worse sinners than all other men who dwelt in Jerusalem? ⁵I tell you, no....* [Though the glory of God is not here mentioned, it is clear that their deaths were not due to greater sin than others. We must not judge others.]

John 9:2–3

When Jesus saw a man blind from birth, his disciples wanted to know who had sinned. *²And his disciples asked Him, saying, "Rabbi, who sinned, this man or his parents, that he was born blind?" ³Jesus answered, "Neither this man nor his parents sinned, but that the works of God should be revealed in him."*

John 11:3–4, 15, 40

³Therefore the sisters [i.e., the sisters of Lazarus] *sent to Him, saying, "Lord, behold, he whom You love is sick." ⁴When Jesus heard that, he said, "This sickness is not unto death, but for the glory of God, that the Son of God may be glorified through it. ¹⁵And I am glad for your sakes that I was not there, that you may believe..." ⁴⁰Jesus said to her, "Did I not say to you that if you would believe you would see the glory of God?"*

2 Corinthians 12:7–10

Though Paul recognized Satan's involvement in his thorn in the flesh, he also recognized God's hand and purpose. After God promised His sufficient grace, Paul said: *⁹...Therefore most gladly I will rather boast in my infirmities, that the power of Christ may rest upon me.*

Hebrews 12:6

For whom the Lord loves He chastens, and scourges every son whom He receives. (See also Revelation 3:19.)

James 3:6

And the tongue is a fire, a world of iniquity. The tongue is so set among our members that it defiles the whole body, and sets on fire the course of nature; and it is set on fire by hell.

A. T. Robertson points out that *defileth* refers to the action of the adrenal glands in stirring up the whole body, affecting digestion, respiration, circulation, etc. Francis W. Dixon writes of a woman's experience with a skin rash. It became so serious that she consulted a specialist, who was unable to determine the cause. On a later visit, she exploded in an expression of hatred for the woman next door. The doctor then diagnosed the problem, saying that when she settled with her neighbor, she would probably find the rash would disappear. It did.

---

2.   Treatment and healing of disease

---

a. Physicians and medicines have a rightful place in healing.

2 Kings 20:1–7

King Hezekiah was sick unto death. God promised restoration, in response to the prayer of Hezekiah, but Isaiah directed in the use of a fig poultice, and Hezekiah recovered. (See also Isaiah 38:21.)

Isaiah 1:6

The description of wounds and bruises here is figurative, picturing the sinfulness of the nation Judah; however, the implication is that a wound that has been bound up and mollified with ointment is better than an open wound.

Jeremiah 8:22

Here, too, the figurative language pictures God's people Judah away from Him. The implication is that since there is available help, there should be healing, but there is no healing. *Is there no balm in Gilead, is there no physician there? Why then is there no recovery for the health of the daughter of my people?*

Jeremiah 30:13

A similar message: *There is no one to plead your cause, that you may be bound up; you have no healing medicines.*

Jeremiah 46:11

This lament was spoken to Egypt. Their sinfulness was so serious to God, that though they would seek help, as one seeks help from medicines, they would not find it.

Ezekiel 47:12 and Revelation 22:2

Part of the description of the New Jerusalem yet to come: *¹²Along the bank of the river...all kinds of trees used for food...They will bear fruit every month, because their water flows from the sanctuary. Their fruit will be for food, and their leaves for medicine.*

Matthew 9:12; See also Mark 2:17 and Luke 5:31

Jesus' testimony as to the need of physicians: *¹²Those who are well have no need of a physician, but those who are sick.*

Luke 10:34

The Good Samaritan bound up the wounds and poured in oil and wine to disinfect and promote healing.

Colossians 4:14

Paul speaks with appreciation of the fact that Luke, the beloved physician, is with him.

b. God both prevents and heals disease, sometimes in answer to prayer, sometimes without our asking.

Exodus 15:26

God promised the Israelites that if they would obey Him, He would make a difference between them and the Egyptians, from whom they had just been delivered. *²⁶And* [the Lord] *said, "If you diligently heed the voice of the Lᴏʀᴅ your God* and do what is right in His sight, give ear to His commandments and keep all His statutes, I will put none of the diseases on you which I have brought on the Egyptians. For I am the LORD who heals you."

Numbers 5:11–28

God can control the effect of drinking polluted water. Here, it was God who directed in a test for adultery.

Deuteronomy 34:7

God gave special physical health and stamina to Moses: *Moses was one hundred and twenty years old when he died. His eyes were not dim nor his natural vigor abated.*

Joshua 14:7–12

God also gave Caleb unusual strength, even in old age: [7][Caleb speaking] *I was forty years old when Moses the servant of the LORD sent me from Kadesh Barnea to spy out the land, and I brought back word to him as it was in my heart. [10]And now, behold, the LORD has kept me alive, as He said, these forty-five years...and now, here I am this day, eighty-five years old. [11]As yet I am as strong this day as I was on the day that Moses sent me; just as my strength was then, so now is my strength for war, both for going out and for coming in. [12]Now therefore give me this mountain, of which the LORD spoke in that day....*

2 Kings 5:1–15

Naaman was healed, encouraged by the faith of a little girl who knew about Elisha, and the reprimand of his servants, who challenged him to obey the prophet, even though Elisha's direction did not please him.

Isaiah 29:18

Referring to the Kingdom Age: *In that day the deaf shall hear the words of the book, and the eyes of the blind shall see out of obscurity and out of darkness.*

Isaiah 35:5–6

Also referring to the Kingdom: [5]*Then the eyes of the blind shall be opened, and the ears of the deaf shall be unstopped. [6]Then the lame shall leap, like a deer, and the tongue of the dumb sing....*

Matthew 4:23–24

[23]*Now Jesus went about all Galilee, teaching*

...*preaching...and healing all kinds of sickness and all kinds of disease among the people. [24]Then His fame went throughout all Syria; and they brought to Him all sick people who were afflicted with various diseases and torments, and those who were demon-possessed, epileptics, and paralytics; and He healed them.*

PROJECT: Study the following references to the healing ministry of Jesus while on earth in a human body. In each case, note whether a sufferer asked to be healed, or whether someone else asked in his behalf, or whether no one asked. Note also the variety of ailments. God's power is not limited!

Matthew 8:5–10, 14–17; 9:2–8, 20–22, 27–30, 32–35; 12:9–13, 22; 14:35–36; 15:30–31; 17:14–21; 20:30–34.

Mark 1:23–27, 29–31, 32–34, 40–45; 2:3–12; 3:1–5; 5:1–19, 22–43; 7:24–30, 32–37; 8:22–26; 10:46–52.

Luke 4:33–37, 38–41; 5:12–15, 17–26; 6:6–11; 7:2–10, 11–16; 8:2, 26–36, 41–42, 43–48, 49–56; 14:2–6; 18:35–43; 22:47–51.

John 4:46–54, 5:1–9, 9:1–7, 11:1–44.

c.   In the Apostolic Period of the history of the church, God gave the gift of healing to a limited group, as a witness to the truth of the Gospel.

Matthew 10:1, 8; Mark 6:7, 13; Luke 9:1–6

Here are three accounts of Jesus sending out the Twelve, directing them, among other things, to heal the sick, cleanse the leper, raise the dead, cast out demons. He gave them power and authority over all devils (or demons), and to cure diseases.

Luke 10:1, 9

A bit later, He sent out the Seventy; they too were told to heal the sick.

Mark 16:17–18, 20

In Mark's account of the commission given to the Eleven, after the resurrection, Jesus said, [17]*And these signs will follow those who believe: In My name they will cast out demons; they will speak with new tongues; [18]They will take up serpents; and if they drink anything deadly, it will by no means hurt them; they will lay hands on the sick, and they will recover. It happened as He had promised....* *[20]And they went out and preached everywhere, the Lord working with them and confirming the word through the accompanying signs.*

Hebrews 2:3–4

Here is the explanation of the giving of the special gifts to these special people: *[3]How shall we escape, if we neglect so great a salvation; which at the first began to be spoken by the Lord, and was confirmed to us by those who heard Him; [4]God also bearing witness both with signs and wonders, with various miracles, and gifts of the Holy Spirit, according to His own will?*

PROJECT: Study the commands of Christ made after the Resurrection to find out what is included in them. What does He command? Note Matthew 28:18–20; Mark 16:15; Luke 24:47–48; Acts 1:8; study also the commands and exhortations given in the various Epistles, looking for commands for believers today.

PROJECT: Study the following passages in the Book of Acts. All refer to healing in some way. Note what persons used the gift of healing, what were the circumstances, and what were the results beyond the healing itself. Acts 3:1–11; 4:29–31; 5:12, 15–16; 14:8–18; 16:16–24; 19:11–18; 28:3–6, 7–10.

---

d. God tells us to pray for our own healing, and for the healing of others, but He does not heal every ailment.

Numbers 21:6–9

Israel sinned in murmuring against God and speaking against Moses, His appointed leader. God sent fiery serpents whose bite brought death to many people. They recognized their sin and acknowledged it to Moses, saying, *[7]...Pray to the LORD, that He take away the serpents from us. So Moses prayed for the people. [8]Then the LORD said to Moses, "Make a fiery serpent...everyone who is bitten, when he looks at it, shall live."*

2 Kings 20:1–7; Isaiah 38:1–5

King Hezekiah of Judah was seriously ill. Isaiah brought a message from God that he would die. Hezekiah prayed; Isaiah returned with a new message that he would be healed and would live for another fifteen years.

2 Chronicles 16:12

A contrast with Hezekiah's experience. King Asa became severely ill with his feet. Though he was exceedingly ill, apparently over a two year period, *in his disease he did not seek the LORD, but the physicians.* As a result he died.

John 11:1–6

Lazarus was sick; his sisters sent for Jesus, knowing that He could heal their brother if he would. *[6]So, when He heard that he was sick, He stayed two more days in the place where He was.*

Meanwhile Lazarus died. Yet Jesus had said, *[4]This sickness is not unto death, but for the glory of God, that the Son of God might be glorified through it.* [Jesus had bigger plans than the healing of Lazarus; He raised him from the dead, even after four days!]

2 Corinthians 12:8–10

Paul had some physical problem, which he called his thorn in the flesh. Apparently he was seriously concerned about his condition, for he says: *[8]Concerning this thing I pleaded with the Lord three times that it might depart from me. [9]And he said to me, "My grace is sufficient for you, for My strength is made perfect in weakness." Therefore most gladly I will rather boast in my infirmities, that the power of Christ may rest upon me.*

Philippians 2:25–30

Epaphroditus was Paul's *brother, and companion in labor, and fellow worker,* and the messenger of the Philippian church who had brought him their gift of love. He was sick, *almost unto death, but God had mercy on him.* He was also greatly concerned that the believers would worry about him since they had heard of his illness. *God had mercy on him,* and on Paul, and gave healing, at least in measure.

1 Timothy 5:23

The Apostle Paul was concerned for Timothy's stomach trouble, whatever it was, and recommended a little wine, rather than water. He did not heal him, as far as we know.

2 Timothy 4:20

Paul, in writing to Timothy, explains, *²⁰Trophimus have I left at Miletum sick.*

James 5:13–16

¹³Is anyone among you suffering? Let him pray.... ¹⁴Is anyone among you sick? Let him call for the elders of the church, and let them pray over him, anointing him with oil in the name of the Lord: ¹⁵And the prayer of faith will save the sick, and the Lord will raise him up. And if he has committed sins, he will be forgiven.

---

3. Specific diseases and deformities mentioned in the Bible

For a study of specific diseases, consult a Bible encyclopedia. The following references from the King James Bible may be of interest.

Ague: Leviticus 26:16

Atrophy: Matthew 12:10–13; Mark 3:1–6; Luke 6:6–11

Blain: Exodus 9:9–10

Blemish: Leviticus 21:17–23; of animals, Leviticus 22:19–25

Blindness: Genesis 19:11; Leviticus 21:18; Deuteronomy 28:28; 2 Kings 6:18–23; Matthew 9:27–30, 11:5, 12:22, 20:30–34, 21:14; Mark 8:22–25, 10:46–52; John 9:1–7; Acts 9:8–9, 13:11. Also the following instances: Genesis 27:1, 48:10; 1 Samuel 4–15; 1 Kings 14:4

Boils: Exodus 9:9, 10; Leviticus 13:18–23; 2 Kings 20:7; Isaiah 38:21; Job 2:7–8

Consumption: Leviticus 26:16; Deuteronomy 28:22

Deafness: Exodus 4:11; Leviticus 19:14; Matthew 11:5; Mark 7:32, 9:25

Dropsy: Luke 14:2

Dyspepsia: 1 Timothy 5:23

Fever: Leviticus 16:16; Deuteronomy 28:22; Job 30:30; Psalm 22:15; Matthew 8:14; Acts 28:8

Hemorrhage: Matthew 9:20; Mark 5:25; Luke 8:43

Hemorrhoids: 1 Samuel 5:6, 12; Deuteronomy 28:27

Inflammation: Leviticus 13:28; Deuteronomy 28:22

Insanity: Deuteronomy 28:28; Proverbs 26:18; Daniel 4:32–34; Zechariah 12:4; Matthew 4:24, 17:15

Itch: Deuteronomy 28:27

Lameness: Leviticus 21:18; 2 Samuel 5:8, 9:3; Matthew 11:5, 15:31, 21:14; Luke 7:22; Acts 3:2–11

Leprosy: Leviticus 13:13–14, 22:4; Numbers 5:1–3, 12:1–14; Deuteronomy 24:8; 2 Kings 5:1-19, 27; 7:3–11; 15:5; 2 Chronicles 26:20–23; Matthew 8:2–4; Mark 1:40–45, 14:3; Luke 5:12–13, 17:12–19

Paralysis, palsy: Matthew 4:24; 8:6, 13; 9:2, 6; Acts 8:7, 9:33–34

Scab, a skin disease: Leviticus 13:2–8, 14:56, 21:20, 22:22; Deuteronomy 28:27; Isaiah 3:17

Scurvy: Leviticus 22:22

Speech impediment: Exodus 4:10; Isaiah 32:4, 33:19; Matthew 9:32–33, 12:22, 15:30–31; Mark 7:37; 9:17, 25–26, Luke 1:20, 64

IV. MENTAL AND EMOTIONAL HEALTH

---

1. A variety of factors may contribute to emotional problems.

---

a. Poor physical health may cause emotional problems, or contribute to them.

Examples:

1 Kings 19:1–4

A combination of exhaustion, lack of food, and fear on the heels of a great victory on Mount Carmel, with all of the emotional excitement attached to that victory, brought the prophet Elijah to the juniper tree experience, where he wished to die.

Job 3:3–21

Though Job did not curse God but continued to trust Him, he was depressed, and expressed his feelings in numerous ways. For example: *³"May the day perish on which I was born, and the night in which it was said, 'A male child is conceived'... ⁹May the stars of its morning be dark; may it look for light, but have none, and not see the dawning of the day; ¹⁰Because it did not shut up the doors of my mother's womb, nor hide sorrow from my eyes. ¹¹Why did I not die at birth? Why did I not perish when I came from the womb?... ²⁰Why is light given to him who is in misery, and life to the bitter of soul; ²¹Who long for death, but it does not come, and search for it more than hidden treasures....* (See also 6:8–9.)

He had lost his ten children, 11,500 animals, his staff of servants, and now was covered with *painful boils from the sole of his foot to the crown of his head.* (Job 1:13–19, 2:7).

b. Circumstances may be so overwhelming as to cause serious problems.

Job 1:13–22, 2:7–8; Job 29–30

Job 1 and 2 describe the circumstances, the losses that Job experienced in a very short time. Job 29–30 shows the effect of both the disease and the other losses on Job's thinking, his self–image, and his sense of helplessness and hopelessness. He contrasts here his former prosperous days when everyone looked up to him and respected him, and his present life when those who are younger taunt him constantly.

Lamentations

Most of this book is made up of lamentations expressing Jeremiah's extreme sorrow for the condition of his people as a result of their sin.

c. Satanic or demonic activity may be a factor in emotional problems.

1 Samuel 16:14–15, 18:10, 19:9

An evil spirit entered into King Saul, making him so jealous of David that he tried three times to kill him, and once to kill his son Jonathan.

Job 1:8–12, 2:1–8

Behind all of Job's losses was the action of Satan. Yet we should be aware of the fact that even his activity was within the bounds that God had set.

Matthew 8:28–34; Mark 5:1–21; Luke 8:26–40

Two men in the country of the Gergesenes met Jesus. They were possessed with demons; they were fierce, uncontrollable, cutting their own bodies, naked, living in tombs.

Matthew 15:22–29; Mark 7:25–30

Along the coast between Tyre and Sidon, Jesus encountered a woman who begged Him to heal her daughter because she was grievously vexed with a demon.

Matthew 17:14–18; Mark 9:17–27; Luke 9:37–43

Here was a man seeking help for his son whom he described as an *epileptic and suffers severely.* So serious was his state that he often fell into the fire or into water; he foamed at the mouth and gnashed with his teeth—all because of an evil spirit.

d. God may judge sin by imposing a mental condition in which one is out of touch with reality.

Daniel 4:28–34

King Nebuchadnezzar of Babylon looked over his kingdom and took credit for its size and prosperity, claiming it was all in his honor. God spoke and announced that the kingdom would be removed from him, and that he would behave as an animal until he should come to recognition of the Most High God.

Deuteronomy 28:28

God had earlier said to Israel that if they refused to hearken to Him (v. 15). *The Lord will strike you with madness and blindness and confusion of heart.*

Zechariah 12:4

God, in describing the Day of the Lord, yet future, said, *"In that day,"* says the Lord, *"I will strike every horse with confusion, and its rider with madness...."*

e. Guilt over sin and failure to accept God's forgiveness may be the cause of severe depression.

Romans 7:15–25; 8:1

Paul describes his experience in which he recognizes his sins and laments over his failure to do what God desires. Finally he sees deliverance through Jesus Christ, and in 8:1 proclaims: *There is therefore now no condemnation to those who are in Christ Jesus....*

f. God's refining process may necessitate our passing through some difficult places and even some low times emotionally.

Genesis 32:24–32

Jacob had gone his own way for a long time; now he spent a night wrestling with the man of God. This was a crisis in his life and resulted in his knowing God better. It was not however a joyful occasion while it was happening.

Job 1:8, 12; 2:3, 6; 42:1–6, 10–17

It was God who initiated the conversation with Satan saying, *8Have you considered My servant Job, that there is none like him on the earth, a blameless and upright man, one who fears God and shuns evil?* Later God challenged Satan again, repeating His evaluation of Job and adding, *3...And still he holds fast his integrity, although you incited Me against him, to destroy him without cause.* In the end, Job testified that, through all of his questioning and his unpleasant experience, he had come to know the Lord more completely. *42:5I have heard of You by the hearing of the ear, but now my eye sees You. 6Therefore I abhor myself, and repent in dust and ashes.... 10And the LORD restored Job's losses when he prayed for his friends. Indeed the LORD gave Job twice as much as he had before.*

Romans 8:18

For I consider that the sufferings of this present time are not worthy to be compared with the glory which shall be revealed in us.

PROJECT: Study the following passages, each describing the encounter of a man with God, and the call of God for him to do some particular task. Note the attitude of each of the men, his feeling of unworthiness and inability, and God's assurance of His sufficiency. Exodus 4:1–18; Joshua 5:13–15; Isaiah 6:1–13; Jeremiah 1:4–19; Ezekiel 1:28 and 2:1–11; Daniel 10; Acts 9:1–19; Revelation 1:9–19. Not all of God's dealings with His people result in emotional highs.

"In sickness let me not so much say, am I getting better of my pain? as am I getting better for it?"
—William Shakespeare (1564–1616).

2. God intends that, in general, a joyful and optimistic spirit should characterize believers.

Psalm 23:1

The LORD is my shepherd. I shall not want. The whole Psalm is relevant. So are many of the Psalmist's statements, such as Psalm 4:8.

Psalm 27:1

The LORD is my light and my salvation: Whom shall I fear? The LORD is the strength of my life; of whom shall I be afraid?

Psalm 34:4

I sought the LORD, and He heard me, and delivered me from all my fears.

Psalm 56:3–4

3Whenever I am afraid, I will trust in You. 4In God (I will praise His word), In God I have put my trust; I will not fear. What can flesh do to me?

Psalm 144:15

Happy are the people who are in such a state; Happy are the people whose God is the LORD.

Psalm 147:3–5

3He heals the brokenhearted And binds up their wounds. 4He counts the number of the stars; He calls them all by name. 5Great is our LORD, and mighty in power; His understanding is infinite.

Proverbs 14:26

In the fear of the LORD there is strong confidence, and His children will have a place of refuge.

Proverbs 17:22

A merry heart does good, like medicine, but a broken spirit dries the bones.

Isaiah 26:3–4

3You will keep him in perfect peace, whose mind is stayed on You, because he trusts in You. 4Trust in the LORD forever, for in YAH, the LORD, is everlasting strength.

Isaiah 30:15

God's word to Israel in a crisis time has application also to present–day believers: *In quietness and confidence shall be your strength.*

Matthew 6:25–34

33But seek first the kingdom of God, and His righteousness; and all these things shall be added to you. 34Therefore do not worry about tomorrow, for tomorrow will worry about its own things. Sufficient for the day is its own trouble.

1 Corinthians 13:4–8

The description of love given here is one that pictures contentment with what God has given, willingness to see the best, looking for that which is better in the future.

1 Corinthians 14:33

For God is not the author of confusion, but of peace, as in all churches of the saints. Though here the primary reference is to lack of confusion in the church, God is not the author of confusion in lives either.

Galatians 5:22–23

22But the fruit of the Spirit is love, joy, peace, longsuffering, kindness, goodness, faithfulness, 23Gentleness, self–control. Against such there is no law.

Philippians 4:11–12

Paul's testimony written from prison: *11Not that I speak in regard to need, for I have learned in whatever state I am, to be content. 12I know how to be abased, and I know how to abound. Everywhere and in all things I have learned both to be full and to be hungry, both to abound and to suffer need.*

Colossians 3:15

And let the peace of God rule in your hearts, to which also you were called in one body; and be thankful.

2 Timothy 1:7

For God has not given us a spirit of fear; but of power, and of love, and of a sound mind.

1 John 4:18–19

18There is no fear in love; but perfect love casts out fear, because fear involves torment. But he who fears has not been made perfect in love. 19We love Him, because He first loved us.

---

3. Confidence and strength depend on a proper trust in the Lord and in His promises.

Many of the passages listed in the preceeding section also apply to this concept. Note especially Psalm 23; Proverbs 14:26; Isaiah 26:3–4; Matthew 6:25–34; 2 Timothy 1:7; 1 John 4:18–19. In addition, here are a few of the precious promises, which are but samples of all God has for believers.

Proverbs 3:5–6, 9–10

5Trust in the LORD with all thine heart; and lean not to thine own understanding. 6In all your ways acknowledge Him, and He shall direct your paths,... 9Honor the LORD with your possessions, and with the firstfruits of all your increase: 10So your barns will be filled with plenty, and your vats will overflow with new wine.

Philippians 4:5–9

5Let your gentleness be known to all men. The Lord is at hand. 6Be anxious for nothing, but in everything by prayer and supplication, with thanksgiving, let your requests be made known to God. 7And the peace of God, which surpasses all understanding, will guard your hearts and minds through Christ Jesus. 8Finally, brethren, whatever things are true, whatever things are noble, whatever things are just, whatever things are pure, whatever things are lovely, whatever things are of good report, if there is any virtue and if there is anything praiseworthy—meditate on these things. 9The things which you learned and received and heard and saw in me, these do, and the God of peace will be with you.

1 Peter 5:7

Casting all your care upon Him; for He cares for you.

---

4. Discerning and considerate friends are valuable assets in times of mental and emotional distress.

Job 6:14–15

In the preceding verses Job expresses his discouragement and even his wish that God would take his life. His friends have been no help. So he says: *14To him who is afflicted, kindness should be shown by his friend, even though he forsakes the fear of the Almighty. 15My brothers have dealt deceitfully like a brook, like the streams of the brooks that pass away.* [NASB] *14For the despairing man there should be kindness from his friend; Lest he forsake the fear of the Almighty.*

Psalm 55:4–6, 12–14

David describes his despair and then his disappointment in betrayal by the friend from whom he had expected help and encouragement. *4My heart is severely pained...terrors of death... 5Fearfulness and trembling have come upon me, and horror has overwhelmed me. 6And I said, "Oh that I had wings like a dove! for then would I fly away, and be at rest...." 12For it is not an enemy who reproaches me; Then I could bear it. Nor is it one who hates me who has magnified himself against me; Then I could hide from him: 13But it was you, a man my equal, my companion and my acquaintance. 14We took sweet counsel together, and walked to the house of God in the throng.* (See also Psalm 41:9.)

Proverbs 11:13–14

13A talebearer reveals secrets, but he who is of a faithful spirit conceals a matter... 14Where there is no counsel, the people fall; but in the multitude of counselors there is safety.

Proverbs 17:9, 17

9He who covers a transgression seeks love, but he who repeats a matter separates the best of friends. 17A friend loves at all times....

Proverbs 27:17

Iron sharpens iron; so a man sharpens the countenance of his friend.

1 Corinthians 13:4–8

4Love suffers long, and is kind...does not envy...does not parade itself, is not puffed up, 5...is not provoked, think no evil; 6does not rejoice in iniquity... 7Bears all things, believes all things, hopes...endures all things.

James 5:13–18

13Is anyone among you suffering? Let him pray... 14Is anyone among you sick? Let him call for the elders of the church, and let them pray over him, anointing him with oil in the name of the Lord: 15And the prayer of faith will save the sick, and the Lord will raise him up;... 16Pray for one another, that you may be healed. The effective, fervent prayer of a righteous man avails much. God directs that in the church we should be concerned about one another in times of trial.

V. THE HANDICAPPED

Note: Many aspects of this subject are considered in the section of this chapter, entitled "Disease and Healing." The following specific thoughts may be helpful.

1. God made man's body, even with its handicaps and limitations.

Exodus 4:10–11

The conversation of God and Moses at the burning bush: *10Then Moses said to the LORD, "O my Lord, I am not eloquent, neither before nor since You have spoken to Your servant; but I am slow of speech and slow of tongue." 11So the LORD said to him, "Who has made man's mouth? Or who makes the mute, the deaf, the seeing, or the blind? Have not I, the LORD?"*

Proverbs 20:12

The hearing ear, and the seeing eye, the LORD has made both of them.

2. God sometimes has a special purpose in a handicap, which may or may not be known to the person involved.

Genesis 19:11

When the men of Sodom came to Lot's door and were about to break it down in order to reach the two angels who had come to rescue Lot and his family from the destruction of Sodom, and to involve them in homosexuality, the angels struck the Sodomites with blindness, so they could not find the door.

Deuteronomy 28:28

In God's list of judgments which He would send upon Israel if they refused to obey Him and honor Him, He said, *28The LORD will strike you with madness and blindness and confusion of heart: 29And you shall grope at noonday, as a blind man gropes in darkness; you shall not prosper in your ways...* Though spiritual blindness is undoubtedly involved here, it is evident from earlier verses that physical judgment is included.

2 Kings 6:18–23

When Syria was after Elisha, Elisha asked the Lord to smite the Syrian army with blindness; then he led them to Samaria to the king of Israel as captives.

Matthew 11:2–5, 15:31; Luke 7:22

Here, Jesus used the healing of the blind, the lame, the lepers, the deaf and the dead as a sign of His identity.

Luke 4:18

When Jesus read from the Law in the synagogue in Nazareth, he read from Isaiah 61:1 and identified Himself with this prophecy which, among other things, said that, as the anointed of the Lord, He would restore sight to the blind.

John 9:2–3 (Read the whole chapter.)

²And His disciples asked Him, saying, "Rabbi, who sinned, this man or his parents, that he was born blind?" ³Jesus answered, "Neither this man nor his parents sinned, but that the works of God should be revealed in him."

Acts 3:2–11

A lame man, crippled from birth, was healed through the ministry of Peter and John. The result was: *⁸So he, leaping up, stood and walked and entered the temple with them—walking, leaping, and praising God. ⁹And all the people saw him walking and praising God. ¹⁰...and they were filled with wonder and amazement at what had happened to him.* The result was an unusual opportunity to preach Christ.

Acts 9:8–18

Saul was made blind for three days at the time of his conversion. The reason is not given in Scripture whether the blindness was a way of getting his attention, or a sign to convince believers that something significant had really happened to change him.

Acts 13:10–11

When Elymas the sorcerer attempted to turn his superior, Deputy Sergius Paulus, away from the Gospel he desired to believe, Paul said, *¹⁰"...O full of all deceit and all fraud, you son of the devil, you enemy of all righteousness, will you not cease perverting the straight ways of the Lord? ¹¹And now, indeed, the hand of the Lord is upon you, and you shall be blind, not seeing the sun for a time."* And immediately a dark mist fell on him, and he went around seeking someone to lead him by the hand.

---

3. God is not limited in His ability to heal or to restore, though He does not always choose to do so.

See previous section, "Disease and Healing."

---

4. The Bible records many kinds of handicaps that existed in Bible times.

PROJECT: Use a Bible concordance to find specific references to blindness, deafness, dumbness, or speech impediment, left-handedness, lameness, demon possession, chronic illness of various kinds. See earlier list. In some cases a topical Bible will list passages which do not contain the specific name of the disability, but describe it. *Nave's Topical Bible* is an old standard reference book which should be in your school or church library.

---

5. God expects us to be considerate of those with handicaps.

Leviticus 19:14

You shall not curse the deaf, nor put a stumbling block before the blind, but shall fear your God: I am the LORD.

Deuteronomy 27:18

Moses charged the Levites and the people of Israel that God's blessings and cursings should be shouted from Mt. Ebal and Mt. Gerizim. Among the statements to be included is this one: *¹⁸"'Cursed is the one who makes the blind to wander off the road.' And all the people shall say, 'Amen!'"*

Job 29:15

In Chapter 1 and 2, God testifies to Job's godliness. In this chapter, he rehearses some of the details of his righteousness and of the things that he had done that made people respect him. Among them: *I was eyes to the blind, and I was feet to the lame.*

Ephesians 4:32

This verse epitomizes what is also said in many other places, that as believers we are to be concerned about people and their needs. *And be kind to one another, tenderhearted, forgiving one another, just as God in Christ also forgave you.*

1 John 2:6

Jesus, in His life on earth, showed compassion for those with handicaps of various kinds. So ought we. *He who says he abides in Him ought himself also to walk just as He walked.*

6. God can use people in spite of handicaps.

Examples:

Exodus 4:10–12

¹⁰Then Moses said to the Lord "...I am not eloquent...I am slow of speech, and slow of tongue." ¹¹So the Lord said to him... ¹²"Now therefore go, and I will be with your mouth and teach you what you shall say." Moses was surely not eager, but together with Aaron, God mightily used him.

2 Kings 7:1–15

Four lepers, ostracized from the camp of Israel, dared to scout the Syrian army camp, recognizing the fact that they might be taken as prisoners, or might be killed. They found it empty of men, but full of supplies which Israel desperately needed. They reported what they found to the gatekeepers, since they could not enter themselves. The message was carried to the king, who found that the report was true.

2 Corinthians 12:7–9

God promised Paul, in answer to his thrice repeated request for deliverance from his thorn in the flesh, *⁹...My grace is sufficient for You: for My strength is made perfect in weakness. Paul's response: ...Therefore most gladly I will rather boast in my infirmities, that the power of Christ may rest upon me.*

VI. PUBLIC HEALTH

Though most of the public health instructions of the Bible are specifically directed to Israel and are designed to emphasize the special nature of the Jewish people as a people chosen by God for a particular purpose, they do have significance today. Modern research by medical doctors bears out the value of God's health laws.

> *"I never drink...I cannot do it on equal terms with others...It costs them only one day, but it costs me three; the first in sinning, the second in suffering, and the third in repenting."*
> —Lawrence Sterne (1713–1768), English clergy.

1. Diet and foods

a. Meat should be carefully selected with particular avoidance of scavenger animals.

Leviticus 11:1–30, 41–43

Here are listed the clean and the unclean animals, a careful study of which indicates that these are animals which feed on dead bodies, or are in other ways scavengers. (See also Deut. 14.)

Leviticus 17:15

And every person who eats what died naturally or what was torn by beasts, whether he is a native of your own country or a stranger, he shall both wash his clothes and bathe in water, and be unclean until evening...

b. Blood should be drained from meat before it is eaten.

Genesis 9:3–4

³Every moving thing that lives shall be food for you,... ⁴But you shall not eat flesh with its life, that is, its blood.

Leviticus 7:26–27

²⁶Moreover you shall not eat any blood in any of your dwellings, whether of bird or beast. ²⁷Whoever eats any blood, that person shall be cut off from his people.

Leviticus 17:10–14

¹³And whatever man of the children of Israel, or of the strangers who sojourn among you, who hunts and catches any animal or bird that may be eaten, he shall pour out its blood and cover it with dust. (See also Deuteronomy 12:23–25.)

NOTE: More recent studies have shown that blood is an excellent medium for the growth and multiplication of bacteria.

c. Animal fat should be avoided.

Leviticus 7:23–25

²³Speak to the children of Israel, saying, "You shall not eat any fat, of ox or sheep or goat. ²⁴And the fat of a beast that dies naturally, and the fat of what is torn by wild animals, may be used in any other way; but you shall by no means eat it. ²⁵For whoever eats the fat of the beast of which men offer an offering made by fire to the LORD, the person who eats it shall be cut off from his people."

d. A safe water supply is essential to health.

Exodus 7:20–25

One of the plagues which God sent upon Egypt was the pollution of their water supply, when the waters turned to blood, the fish died and the Egyptians could not drink the water.

Exodus 15:23–27

On the journey from Egypt to Canaan, God's people came to Marah where the waters were bitter and unfit for drinking. In response to Moses' prayer, *²⁵...The LORD showed him a tree, which when he had cast into the waters, the waters were made sweet...It was there too that God made a promise to Israel that depended on their being faithful to Him: ²⁶...I will put none of these diseases on you which I have brought on the Egyptians. For I am the LORD who heals you. ²⁷Then they came to Elim, where there were twelve wells of water and seventy palm trees; so they camped there by the waters.*

> *"The prolongation of life and the reestablishment of health, for which medicine labors with all its strength, are seen to be a blessing from the merciful God, a respite, a stay of execution. We may ask why God grants us this respite. It can only be that He wants us to use it to come nearer to Him, laying hold through faith on His promises of eternal life."*
> —Paul Tournier, A Doctor's Casebook, p. 37.

2. Sanitation

a. Patients with contagious diseases should be isolated.

Leviticus 12:1–13:46

⁴⁶He shall be unclean. All the days he has the sore he shall be unclean. He is unclean, and he shall dwell alone; his habitation shall be outside the camp.

b. Clothing, bed linens, and tensils contaminated by disease must be thoroughly cleansed.

Leviticus 13:47–59; 15:1–13, 19–28, 31

Here, in considerable detail, are instructions concerning a variety of items which may easily be contaminated by disease, and which therefore need cleansing.

c. A house which, after repeated inspection and decontamination, cannot be freed from evidence of disease must be destroyed. (Leviticus 14:34–48.)

d. One who handles dead bodies needs cleansing before resuming his normal activities.

Leviticus 11:31–40

³¹These [previously named animals] are unclean to you among all that creep. Whoever touches them when they are dead shall be unclean until evening. ³⁹And if any beast, of which you may eat dies, he who touches its carcass shall be unclean until evening. ⁴⁰He who eats of its carcass shall wash his clothes and be unclean until evening. He also who carries its carcass shall wash his clothes and be unclean until evening.

Numbers 19:7–16

Here, in the description of the ordinance of the red heifer, each person who touched the dead animal was required to wash himself and his clothes and remain unclean until evening. Also, *¹¹He who touches the dead body of anyone shall be unclean seven days. ¹³Whoever touches the body of anyone who has died, and does not purify himself, defiles the tabernacle of the LORD. That person shall be cut off from Israel...*

e. Human excrement must be disposed of in a way that will not spread contamination.

Deuteronomy 23:12–14

12Also you shall have a place outside the camp, where you may go out. 13And you shall have an implement among your equipment, and when you sit down outside, you shall dig with it and turn and cover your refuse. 14Your God walks in the midst of your camp...therefore your camp shall be holy, that He may see no unclean thing among you, and turn away from you.

f. The discharges from seminal emission and menstruation should not be permitted to come in contact with other people.

See Leviticus 15:16–28, 31–33, especially in the *New American Standard Bible.*

g. Circumcision on the eighth day was prescribed by God for the descendents of Abraham and for any other boy or man born in their homes or bought with money.

Genesis 17:12–14

Part of the Abrahamic Covenant: *12He who is eight days old among you shall be circumcised, every male child in your generations, he who is born in your house or bought with money from any stranger who is not your descendant. 13He who is born in your house and he who is bought with your money must be circumcised, and My covenant shall be in your flesh for an everlasting covenant. 14And the uncircumcised male child, who is not circumcised in the flesh of his foreskin, that person shall be cut off from his people; he has broken My covenant.* (See also Leviticus 12:3.)

For the health significance of circumcision, see S. I. McMillen, *None of These Diseases* (Old Tappan, NJ: Fleming H. Revell, 1963), Chapter 3.

3. The work week. Six days of work plus one day of rest is God's plan for man's needs.

Genesis 2:3

Then God blessed the seventh day and sanctified it, because in it He rested from all His work which God had created and made.

Exodus 16:5, 23–30

When God supplied the manna to Israel, He supplied double on the sixth day, so there would be no gathering on the seventh day.

Exodus 20:8–11

8Remember the Sabbath day, to keep it holy. 9Six days you shall labor and do all your work; 10But the seventh day is the Sabbath of the LORD your God. In it you shall do no work: you, nor your son, nor your daughter, nor your manservant, nor your maidservant, nor your cattle, nor your stranger who is within your gates: 11For in six days the LORD made the heavens and the earth, the sea, and all that is in them, and rested the seventh day. Therefore the LORD blessed the Sabbath day and hallowed it.

Exodus 23:12

Six days you shall do your work, and on the seventh day you shall rest; that your ox...donkey ...son of your maidservant...stranger may be refreshed.

Exodus 34:21

Six days you shall work, but on the seventh day you shall rest; in plowing time and in harvest you shall rest. In other words, even in the busiest times.

Exodus 31:13, 17

God made the Sabbath day a special sign between Himself and Israel, and then gave details concerning the keeping of the day as part of the Law for Israel. *13"Speak also to the children of Israel, saying: 'Surely My Sabbaths you shall keep, for it is a sign between Me and you throughout your generations, that you may know that I am the LORD who sanctifies you [set you apart]. 17It is a sign between Me and the children of Israel forever; for in six days the LORD made the heavens and the earth and on the seventh day He rested and was refreshed.'"* (See also Deuteronomy 5:15; Ezekiel 20:12–13, 16.)

Matthew 12:1–8, 10–14; Mark 2:23–28; Luke 13:10–17, 14:1–6; John 5:10–12, 7:23.

In each of these passages Jesus either healed someone on the sabbath day, or he and his disciples plucked grain to eat, making clear the fact that the sabbath was made for man, and not man for the sabbath (Mark 2:27).

"Every sickness is a crisis of life. Every sick person who calls for our help is one who has suddenly become aware of his fragility of everything that once filled his life...If he has regarded them as duties and blessings sent by God, the sudden stoppage caused by the sickness will be easier to bear; he still has God and will wait upon new blessings from Him... But if, on the other hand, he has made them his gods...then suddenly and tragically he is faced with the true problems of life and of his own life. Sickness sets him face to face with God."

—Paul Tournier, *A Doctor's Casebook,* p. 38.

Sex Education

[Fine Arts/Health]

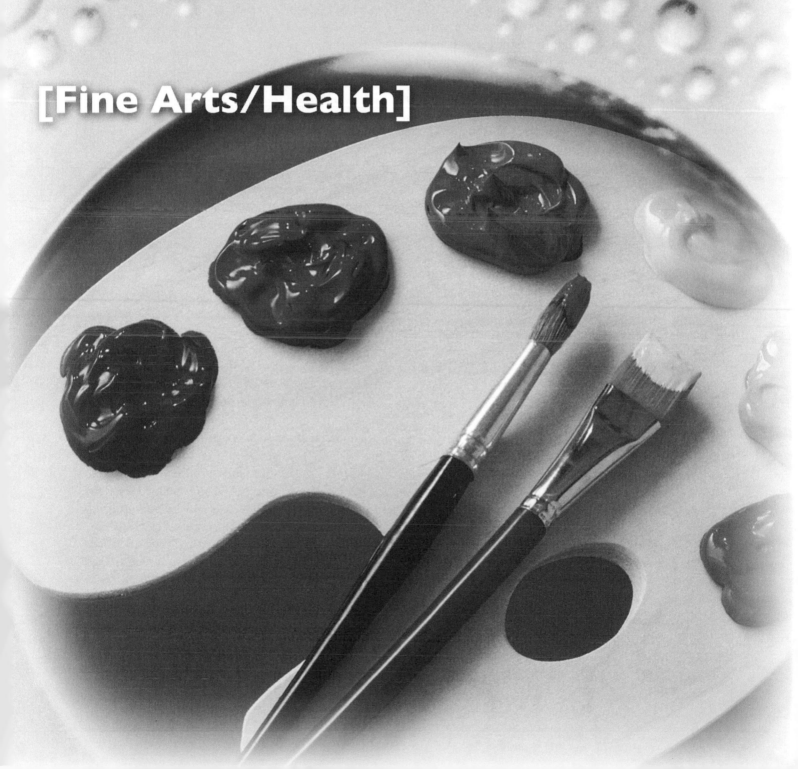

Sex Education: Biblical Concepts

I. SEXUAL ACTIVITY

1. God established marriage to meet the needs of mankind; marriage and sex within marriage are honorable.
2. Sexual activity is to be limited to the marriage relationship.
   a. The union of a man and a woman in marriage is meant to be a picture of the spiritual relationship between Christ and His church.
   b. The standards of morality for believers must come from God, rather than from the unbelieving world.
   c. God specifically condemns various male–female sex acts.
      –incest
      –prostitution
      –rape
   d. God severely judges abnormal or perverted sexual activity.
      –homosexuality
      –bestiality (sexual relation between human and animals)
3. The timing of sexual activity within marriage should be based on concern for mutual needs, both physical and spiritual.
4. God sets high standards for the believer's thought life because thoughts lead to actions.
5. God offers forgiveness for every kind of sin, including that in the sexual realm.

II. PREGNANCY AND CHILDBIRTH

1. God's design for marriage includes the production of children; the desire for children is normal.
2. Pregnancy and childbearing have been affected by sin.
3. God is able to give children even when the physical conditions would make pregnancy and childbirth impossible. God can do miracles.

4. God controls conception.
5. Life begins at conception.
   a. The fetus has individuality, and is known to God as a person.
   b. Under the Law, causing a miscarriage was a punishable offense.

WHAT IS LOVE?

"Love is an image of God, and not a lifeless image, but the living essence of the divine nature which beams full of all goodness."
—Martin Luther (1483–1546), Reformation leader.

"Love never reasons, but profusely gives; gives, like a thoughtless prodigal, its all, and trembles then lest it has done too little."
—Hannah Moore (1745–1843), English author.

"Love...is like a beautiful flower which I may not touch, but whose fragrance makes the garden a place of delight just the same."
—Helen Keller (1880–1968), blind American author.

"Love covers a multitude of sins. When a scar cannot be taken away, the next kind office is to hide it...Love is never so blind as when it is to spy faults...It is like the painter, who,...to draw the picture of a friend having a blemish in one eye, would picture only the other side of his face...It is a noble and great thing to cover the blemishes and to excuse the failings of a friend; to draw a curtain before his stains, and to display his perfections; to bury his weaknesses in silence, but to proclaim his virtues upon the housetop."
—Robert South (1634–1716), English divine.

Sex Education: Biblical Background

> "If a man loves a woman for her beauty, does he love her? No; for the smallpox, which destroys her beauty without killing her, causes his love to cease. And if any one loves me for my judgment or my memory, does he really love me? No; for I can lose these qualities without ceasing to be."
> —Blaise Pascal (1623–1662), French mathematician and philosopher.

> "It seems to me that the coming of love is like the coming of spring—the date is not to be reckoned by the calendar. It may be slow and gradual; it may be quick and sudden. But in the morning, when we wake and recognize a change in the world without, verdure on the trees, blossoms on the sward, warmth in the sunshine, music in the air, we say spring has come."
> —Edward George Bulwer–Lytton (1803–1873), English novelist.

> "Love is like the moon; when it does not increase it decreases."
> —Joseph Alexander Segur (1756–1805), French dramatist.

> "It is astonishing how little one feels poverty when one loves."
> —Edward George Bulwer–Lytton.

> "As every lord giveth a certain livery to his servants, love is the very livery of Christ. Our Savior, who is the Lord above all lords, would have his servants known by their badge, which is love."
> —Hugh Latimer (1490–1555), English Protestant bishop.

I.   SEXUAL ACTIVITY

1.   God established marriage to meet the needs of mankind; marriage and sex within marriage are honorable.

Genesis 2:18, 20–25

[18]And the LORD God said, "It is not good that the man should be alone, I will make him a helper comparable to him." [20]But for Adam there was not found a helper comparable to him. [21]And the LORD God caused a deep sleep to fall on Adam... [22]Then the rib...He made into a woman, and He brought her to the man. [23]And Adam said, "This is now bone of my bones, and flesh of my flesh: she shall be called Woman, because she was taken out of Man." [24]Therefore a man shall leave his father and mother and be joined to his wife, and they shall become one flesh. [25]And they were both naked, the man and his wife, and were not ashamed.

Proverbs 5:18–19

[18]Let your fountain be blessed, and rejoice with the wife of your youth. [19]As a loving deer and a graceful doe, let her breasts satisfy you at all times; and always be enraptured with her love.

Proverbs 18:22

He who finds a wife finds a good thing, and obtains favor from the LORD.

Ecclesiastes 9:9

Live joyfully with the wife whom you love all the days of your vain life which He has given you under the sun....

Song of Solomon

"The interpretation (of this book) is twofold: Primarily, the book is the expression of pure marital love as ordained of God in creation, and the vindication of that love as against both asceticism and lust—the two profanations of the holiness of marriage. The secondary and larger interpretation is of Christ, the Son and His heavenly bride, the Church."
—The Scofield Reference Bible (New York: Oxford University Press, 1909), p. 705.

Matthew 19:4–6; Mark 10:6–9

Here, Jesus reiterates several of the statements from Genesis 2, with emphasis on the two becoming one, leaving parents for one another, a permanent relationship.

1 Corinthians 7:2–3

²Nevertheless, because of sexual immorality, let each man have his own wife, and let each woman have her own husband. ³Let the husband render to his wife the affection due her, and likewise also the wife to her husband.

1 Timothy 4:1–3

¹Now the Spirit expressly says that in latter times some will depart from the faith…. ³Forbidding to marry, and commanding to abstain from foods which God created to be received with thanksgiving by those who believe and know the truth. [Forbidding marriage is departing from the faith.]

1 Timothy 5:14

Paul, in instructing Timothy concerning the care of widows in the church, said, *¹⁴Therefore I desire that the younger widows marry, bear children, manage the house, give no opportunity to the adversary to speak reproachfully.*

Hebrews 13:4

Marriage is honorable among all, and the bed undefiled.

2. Sexual activity is to be limited to the marriage relationship.

Genesis 20:3–7

Before God gave the Law to Israel, the Philistine king, Abimelech, reprimanded Abraham for placing his wife in such a position that Abimelech might have sinned against her.

Genesis 26:9–11

Similarly, about a hundred years later, the heathen king again reproached Isaac for misrepresenting his wife. *¹¹So Abimelech charged all his people, saying, "He who touches this man or his wife shall surely be put to death."*

Genesis 34:7

Jacob's sons were very upset when a Hivite prince, Shechem, defiled their sister Dinah. The prohibition against sex outside of marriage seems

to have been well understood even before God gave the Law.

Exodus 20:14; See also Deuteronomy 5:18

The seventh commandment: *¹⁴You shall not commit adultery.*

Leviticus 18:20

Moreover you shall not lie carnally with your neighbor's wife, to defile yourself with her. (See also 20:10–12.)

Leviticus 19:20

Whoever lies carnally with a woman who is betrothed as a concubine to another man, and who has not at all been redeemed nor given her freedom, for this there shall be scourging…[Even slave girls were protected.]

Deuteronomy 22:20–30

If a woman be found not to be a virgin at the time of her marriage, the Law was clear: *²¹Then they shall bring out the young woman to the door of her father's house, and the men of her city shall stone her to death with stones, because she has done a disgraceful thing in Israel, to play the harlot in her father's house; so you shall put away the evil person from among you. ²²If a man is found lying with a woman married to a husband, then both of them shall die, both the man that lay with the woman, and the woman; so you shall put away the evil person from Israel.* [Details of the Law in other situations follow.]

2 Samuel 11 and 12:1–23

Here are the details of David's sin with Bathsheba, God's judging of that sin, and David's repentance.

Proverbs 5:3–14, 6:23–35, 7:4–27, 9:13–18, 23:26–28

Here are repeated warnings against prostitution and the consequences of sexual activity with a stranger.

Romans 13:9

In his emphasis on the importance of love in the Christian life, Paul repeats those of the commandments that deal with relationships to other people, among them, *You shall not commit adultery.* He ends with the thought that by obeying these commands of God, we show love to others.

1 Corinthians 5:1–11

In the church at Corinth was a man who was guilty of fornication with his father's wife. The church had not taken action in disciplining him, and Paul insists that they must do so (vv. 3–5). In verses 9–11 he reminds them of a previous letter in which he had warned them not to keep company with fornicators who were believers.

1 Corinthians 6:13–20

¹Now the body is not for sexual immorality but for the Lord, and the Lord for the body.... ¹⁵Do you not know that your bodies are members of Christ? Shall I then take the members of Christ and make them members of a harlot? Certainly not. ¹⁶Or do you not know that he who is joined to a harlot is one body with her? For "The two," He says, "shall become one flesh...." ¹⁸Flee sexual immorality. Every sin that a man does is outside the body, but he who commits sexual immorality sins against his own body. ¹⁹Or do you not know that your body is the temple of the Holy Spirit who is in you, whom you have from God, and you are not your own? ²⁰For you were bought at a price; therefore glorify God in your body and in your spirit, which are God's.

Galatians 5:19–21

¹⁹Now the works of the flesh are evident, which are: adultery, fornication, uncleanness, licentiousness... ²¹of which I tell you beforehand, just as I also told you in time past, that those who practice such things will not inherit the kingdom of God.

Ephesians 5:3, 5

³But fornication and all uncleanness, or covetousness, let it not even be named among you, as is fitting for saints.... ⁵For this you know, that no fornicator, unclean person, nor covetous man, who is an idolater, has any inheritance in the kingdom of Christ and God.

Colossians 3:5 (NASB)

Therefore consider the members of your earthly body as dead to immorality, impurity, passion, evil desire, and greed, which amounts to idolatry.

1 Thessalonians 4:3–4

³For this is the will of God, your sanctification: that you should abstain from sexual immorality: ⁴That each of you should know how to possess his own vessel in sanctification and honor.

Hebrews 13:4

...Fornicators and adulterers God will judge.

a. The union of a man and a woman in marriage is meant to be a picture of the spiritual relationship between Christ and His church.

Ephesians 5:23–32

²³For the husband is the head of the wife, as also Christ is head of the church... ²⁴Therefore just as the church is subject to Christ, so let the wives be to their own husbands in everything. ²⁵Husbands, love your wives, just as Christ also loved the church and gave Himself for it;... ²⁹For no one ever hated his own flesh, but nourishes and cherishes it, just as the Lord does the church.... ³¹For this reason a man shall leave his father and mother and be joined to his wife, and the two shall become one flesh. ³²This is a great mystery, but I speak concerning Christ and the church.

b. The standards of morality for believers must come from God, rather than from the unbelieving world.

Leviticus 18:1–5, 24–30

In these verses which precede and follow God's prohibitions against incest, God makes clear the authority upon which the standards for Israel were based: *²Speak to the children of Israel, and say to them, "I am the LORD your God. ³According to the doings of the land of Egypt, where you dwelt, you shall not do, and according to the doings of the land of Canaan, where I am bringing you, you shall not do; nor shall you walk in their ordinances. ⁴You shall observe My judgments and keep My ordinances, to walk in them: I am the LORD your God."* (See also Lev. 20:23.)

Ephesians 4:17–20

¹⁷This I say, therefore, and testify in the Lord, that you should no longer walk as the rest of the Gentiles walk, in the futility of their mind, ¹⁸...alienated from the life of God... ¹⁹Who being past feeling have given themselves over to licentiousness [sensuality], *to work all uncleanness with greediness. ²⁰But you have not so learned Christ.*

1 Thessalonians 4:3–5

³For this is the will of God, your sanctification [your being set apart], that you should abstain from sexual immorality. ⁴That each of you should know how to possess his own vessel in sanctification and honor, ⁵Not in passion of lust, like the Gentiles who do not know God.

c. God specifically condemns various male–female sex acts—incest, prostitution, rape.

Incest

Incest: sexual intercourse between two persons too closely related to be legally married.

Leviticus 18:6–16

⁶None of you shall approach anyone who is near of kin to him, to uncover his nakedness: I am the LORD. In the next verses are listed the following with whom no intercourse is to take place: father, mother, father's wife, sister or half-sister, granddaughter, aunt, daughter-in-law, sister-in-law.

Leviticus 20:11–12, 17–21

¹¹The man who lies with his father's wife has uncovered his father's nakedness; both of them shall surely be put to death. Their blood shall be upon them. ¹²If a man lies with his daughter-in-law, both of them shall surely be put to death. They have committed perversion. Their blood shall be upon them. Verses 17 and 21 cite some additional penalties under the Law: they shall be cut off in the sight of their people (v.17), die childless (v. 21). See also Deuteronomy 22:30; 27:20, 22–23.

Ezekiel 22:11

In listing sins for which Israel was being judged, Ezekiel includes: *One commits abomination with his neighbor's wife; another lewdly defiles his daughter-in-law; and another in you violates his sister, his father's daughter.*

1 Corinthians 5:1

New Testament standards are no different. Paul, writing to the church in Corinth, condemns them for condoning *such sexual immorality as is not even named among the Gentiles—that a man has his father's wife!*

Specific instances of incest are mentioned: Lot, Gen. 19:31–36; Abraham, Gen. 20:1, 13; Nahor, Gen. 11:29; Reuben, Gen. 35:22 and 49:4; Amram, Ex.

6:20; Judah, Gen. 38:16–18 and 1 Chr. 2:4; Amnon, 2 Sam. 13:14; Absalom, 2 Sam. 16:21–22; Herod, Matt. 14:3–4; Mark 6:17–18; Luke 3:19.

Prostitution

Prostitution: sexual intercourse for money or reward.

Leviticus 19:29

Do not prostitute your daughter, to cause her to be a harlot, lest the land fall into harlotry, and the land become full of wickedness.

Leviticus 21:9

The daughter of any priest, if she profanes herself by playing the harlot, she profanes her father. She shall be burned with fire.

Deuteronomy 23:17–18

¹⁷There shall be no ritual harlot of the daughters of Israel, or a perverted one of the sons of Israel. ¹⁸You shall not bring the hire of a harlot or the price of a dog to the house of the LORD your God for any vowed offering, for both of these are an abomination to the LORD your God.

Judges 11:1–3

Here is one result of prostitution: Gilead had a son, Jephthah, by a harlot. Jephthah became a mighty man of valour. However, the legitimate sons of Gilead refused to include him in the inheritance, and he had to flee to another land.

Proverbs 5:3–14

Here is a description of the actions of a prostitute, a warning against becoming involved, and a listing of some of the results: loss of honor, loss of wealth to strangers (children born to the harlot), venereal disease (v.11).

Proverbs 6:23–25

Again a description of the harlot's actions along with some of the adverse results: poverty (v. 26), destruction of his own soul (v. 32), dishonor and reproach that never end (v.33), jealousy, vengeance and blackmail from the harlot's husband (vv. 34–35).

Proverbs 7:1–27; 9:13–18; 23:26–28

Further descriptions of the ways in which a prostitute attracts a man, and further warnings of the dangers.

Hosea 2:13

In this passage, as well as in many others, God uses the relationship of a man and a harlot to picture Israel's unfaithfulness to Him.

Rape

Rape: a forcible violation of women.

Deuteronomy 22:23–29

Under the Law there were differences in the penalty for the rape depending on whether the woman was already betrothed to another man, and on where the rape occurred—whether the woman was close to help. See also Exodus 22:16–17.

d. God severely judges abnormal or perverted sexual activity.

Homosexuality

Homosexuality: sexual relations between persons of the same sex.

Sodomy: unnatural sexual relations, especially between a human being and an animal.

Lesbianism: homosexuality among women.

Genesis 19:5–11

Two angels visited Lot in Sodom; men of the city stormed his house in an attempt to get access to the angels for homosexual gratification. Finally, the angels pulled Lot back into the house and struck the intruders with blindness, so they could not find the door. God judges homosexual activity.

Leviticus 18:22

You shall not lie with a male as with a woman. It is an abomination.

Leviticus 20:13

If a man lies with a male as he lies with a woman, both of them have committed an abomination. They shall surely be put to death. Their blood shall be upon them.

Deuteronomy 23:17

There shall be no...perverted one of the sons of Israel.

Judges 19:22

A Jewish man, traveling with his concubine and a young man, received hospitality from an old man in Gibeah. *22Now as they were enjoying themselves, suddenly certain men of the city, perverted men, surrounded the house and beat on*

the door. They spoke to the master of the house, the old man, saying, "Bring out the man who came to your house, that we may know him carnally." The old man, recognizing the wickedness of what they wanted to do and his responsibility as a host, refused their request, offering instead his own daughter and his guest's concubine. In other words, sodomy was even more serious than multiple rape.

1 Kings 14:24

In the description of Judah's rebellion against God's Law under King Rehoboam are these words of condemnation: *24And there were also perverted persons in the land. They did according to all the abominations of the nations which the LORD had cast out before the children of Israel.*

1 Kings 15:12

Asa became king over Judah and God describes his heart as perfect with the LORD all his days. Among other reforms in his reign: *12And he banished the perverted persons from the land, and removed all the idols that his fathers had made.*

1 Kings 22:43, 46

Jehoshaphat became king after Asa. *43And he walked in all the ways of his father Asa. He did not turn aside from them, doing what was right in the eyes of the LORD... 46And the rest of the perverted persons, who remained in the days of his father Asa, he banished from the land....*

Romans 1:24–32

In the preceding verses God's complaint against mankind is described: men refused to believe what God made obvious in His creation (vv. 19–20); they refused to recognize God and glorify Him and confess that they owed Him anything (v. 21); they placed man and animals in God's place (vv. 23, 25). As a result, God gave them over to vile affections, which are described in vv. 26–32.

26For this cause God gave them up to vile passions. For even their women exchanged the natural use for what is against nature: 27Likewise also the men, leaving the natural use of the woman, burned in their lust for one another, men with men committing what is shameful, and receiving in themselves the penalty of their error which was due.... 32Who knowing the righteous judgment of God, that those who practice such things are worthy of death, not only do the same but also approve of those who practice them.

1 Corinthians 6:9–10

[9]Do you not know that the unrighteous will not inherit the kingdom of God? Do not be deceived. Neither fornicators, nor idolaters, nor adulterers, nor homosexuals, nor sodomites, [10]...will inherit the kingdom of God.

Bestiality

Bestiality: sexual activity of a man or woman with an animal.

Exodus 22:19

Whoever lies with a beast shall surely be put to death.

Leviticus 18:23

Nor shall you mate with any beast, to defile yourself with it. Nor shall any woman stand before a beast to mate with it. It is perversion.

Leviticus 20:15–16

[15]If a man mates with a beast, he shall surely be put to death, and you shall kill the beast. [16]If a woman approaches any beast and mates with it, you shall kill the woman and the beast. They shall surely be put to death. Their blood is upon them. See also Deuteronomy 27:21.

---

3. **The timing of sexual activity within marriage should be based on concern for mutual needs, both physical and spiritual.**

Leviticus 12:1–8, 15:19–33, 18:19

Under the Law, there was to be no intercourse during the wife's menstrual period, when she was hemorrhaging for some other reason, or for a time after childbirth.

Leviticus 20:18 (NASB)

If there is a man who lies with a menstruous woman and uncovers her nakedness, he has laid bare her flow, and she has exposed the flow of her blood; thus both of them shall be cut off from among their people. (See also Ezekiel 18:5–6, 9.)

1 Corinthians 7:3–5

[3]Let the husband render to his wife the affection due her, and likewise also the wife to her husband. [4]The wife does not have authority over

her own body, but the husband does. And likewise the husband does not have authority over his own body, but the wife does. *[5]Do not deprive one another except with consent for a time, that you may give yourselves to fasting and prayer; and come together again so that Satan does not tempt you because of your lack of self–control.*

Ephesians 5:1–2, 18, 21–22, 24–25, 28–29, 33

[1]Therefore be followers of God as dear children; [2]And walk in love, as Christ also has loved us, and given Himself for us... [18]Be filled with the Spirit;... [21]Submitting to one another in the fear of God. [22]Wives, submit to your own husbands, as to the Lord.... [24]Therefore just as the church is subject to Christ, so let the wives be to their own husbands in everything. [25]Husbands, love your wives, just as Christ also loved the church and gave Himself for it;... [28]So husbands ought to love their own wives as their own bodies; he who loves his wife loves himself. [29]For no one ever hated his own flesh, but nourishes and cherishes it, just as the Lord does the church.... [33]Nevertheless let each one of you in particular so love his own wife as himself, and let the wife see that she respects her husband.

---

4. **God sets high standards for the believer's thought life because thoughts lead to actions.**

Exodus 20:17

You shall not covet your neighbor's house; you shall not covet your neighbor's wife, nor his manservant, nor his maidservant, nor his ox, nor his donkey, nor anything that is your neighbor's. See also Deuteronomy 5:21.

2 Samuel 11:2–27, 12:1–15

The sequence that led to David's sin with Bathsheba is worthy of study. It began with his watching Bathsheba as she was bathing, and noting how beautiful she was. Then came adultery, scheming that led to Uriah's death, and subsequent marriage to Bathsheba.

Proverbs 6:23–25

[23]For the commandment is a lamp; and the law is light; reproofs of instruction are the way of life: [24]To keep you from the evil woman, from the flattery tongue of a seductress. [25]Do not lust after

her beauty in your heart, nor let her allure you with her eyelids.

Matthew 5:27–28

27"You have heard that it was said to those of old 'You shall not commit adultery;' 29But I say to you, That whoever looks at a woman to lust for her has already committed adultery with her in his heart."

Matthew 15:19–20

19For out of the heart proceed evil thoughts, murders, adulteries, fornications, thefts, false witness, blasphemies: 20These are the things which defile a man.... (See also Mark 7:21–23.)

Romans 6:11–13

11Likewise you also, reckon yourselves to be dead indeed to sin, but alive to God in Christ Jesus our Lord. 12Therefore do not let sin reign in your mortal body, that you should obey it in its lusts. 13And do not present your members as instruments of unrighteousness to sin, but present yourselves to God as being alive from the dead, and your members as instruments of righteousness to God.

Romans 13:14

But put on the Lord Jesus Christ, and make no provision for the flesh, to fulfill its lusts.

1 Thessalonians 4:3–5

3For this is the will of God, your sanctification: that you should abstain from sexual immorality: 4That each of you should know how to possess his own vessel in sanctification and honor; 5Not in passion of lust....

James 1:14–15

14But each one is tempted when he is drawn away by his own desires and enticed. 15Then when desire has conceived, it gives birth to sin; and sin, when it is full-grown, brings forth death.

1 John 2:15–16

15 Do not love the world or the things in the world. If anyone loves the world, the love of the Father is not in him. 16For all that is in the world, the lust of the flesh, the lust of the eyes, and the pride of life—is not of the Father but is of the world.

> *"What we are afraid to do before men, we should be afraid to think before God."*
> —Beilby Porteus (1731–1808), English bishop.

5. God offers forgiveness for every kind of sin, including that in the sexual realm.

John 8:3–11

Jesus' handling of the woman taken in adultery makes clear the fact that sexual sin is forgivable, though it is not to be condoned.

1 Corinthians 6:9–11

Here is a list of sinners who will not inherit the kingdom of God. Among others, it includes fornicators, adulterers, effeminate, abusers of themselves with mankind. Then come these gracious words. *11And such were some of you. But you were washed, but you were sanctified, but you were justified in the name of the Lord Jesus and by the Spirit of our God.*

1 Timothy 1:8–15

Paul explains that the Law is good if used rightly, and that it is designed especially for the lawless and disobedient, some of whom he lists: ungodly, sinners, unholy and profane, murderers of parents, manslayers, whoremongers, those that defile themselves with mankind, menstealers, liars, perjured persons. In verses 11–15, he exclaims over the glorious gospel which has been committed to him, when he had formerly been guilty of so much.

II. PREGNANCY AND CHILDBIRTH

1. God's design for marriage includes the production of children; the desire for children is normal.

Genesis 4:1, 25

Eve said, when Cain was born, *I have gotten a man from the LORD;* again, after Abel's death, when Seth came, *she named his name Seth: For God, has appointed another seed for me instead of Abel, whom Cain killed....*

Genesis 9:1

After the Flood: *¹So God blessed Noah and his sons, and said to them: "Be fruitful and multiply, and fill the earth"*

Genesis 16:2

Sarah had no children and recognized the fact that it was the Lord who had restrained her from bearing. She was so desirous of children that she (wrongly) urged Abraham to go in unto her maid, Hagar.

Genesis 18:12

When God announced to Abraham that they were to have a son, even in their old age, *Sarah laughed within herself, saying, "After I have grown old, shall I have pleasure, my lord being old also?"* Even at this age, she thought of having a son as pleasure! See also 21:6–7.

Genesis 24:60

When Rebekah's brother and mother blessed her as she was leaving Haran to go with Abraham's servant, to become the bride for Isaac, they said: *⁶⁰Our sister, may you become the mother of thousands of ten thousands, and may your descendants possess the gates of those who hate them.* The greatest wish they could desire for her was the birth of many children.

Genesis 29:31–35; 30:1, 22–24

Jacob had two wives, Leah and Rachel. Rachel was his favorite but she had no children at this time. Each time that Leah gave birth, she looked upon the birth as a blessing, hoping that this one would turn Jacob's love to her. Rachel was so disappointed in her barrenness that she said to Jacob, *Give me children, or else I die.* Both she and Leah, in an effort to have more children, encouraged conception by their maids. Finally, *²²Then God remembered Rachel and God listened to her and opened her womb. ²³And she conceived, and bore a son; and said, "God has taken away my reproach." ²⁴So she called his name Joseph, and said, "The LORD shall add to me another son."*

Genesis 33:4–5

When Esau and Jacob met after many years of separation, Esau asked, *"Who are these with you?" And he said, "The children whom God has graciously given your servant."*

Genesis 48:9

Joseph too credited God with his sons: *These are my sons, whom God has given me in this place.*

Ruth 4:13–15

When Ruth and Boaz had a son, whom they called Obed, both they and the neighbor women recognized this child as a gift from God. *¹⁴Then the women said to Naomi, "Blessed be the LORD, who has not left you this day without a near kinsman; and may his name be famous in Israel. ¹⁵And may he be to you a restorer of life and a nourisher of your old age; for your daughter–in–law, who loves you, who is better to you than seven sons, has borne him."*

1 Samuel 1:2, 5–8, 19–20, 26–28

Hannah wept because she had no children—so much so that her husband was greatly concerned because she would not eat. Finally, in answer to her prayer, *²⁰...Hannah conceived and bore a son, and called his name Samuel, saying, "Because I have asked for him from the LORD."* Later, when she brought Samuel to Eli, she again acknowledged God's goodness, saying, *²⁷For this child I prayed, and the LORD has granted me my petition which I asked of Him: ²⁸Therefore I also have lent him to the LORD; as long as he lives he shall be lent to the LORD.*

Psalm 127:3–5

³Behold, children are a heritage from the LORD, The fruit to the womb is His reward. ⁴Like arrows in the hand of a warrior, So are the children of one's youth. ⁵Happy is the man that has his quiver full of them...

2. Pregnancy and child–bearing have been affected by sin.

Genesis 3:16

To the woman He said: "I will greatly multiply your sorrow and your conception; in pain you shall bring forth children...." This was the result of the sin of Adam and Eve in the garden, and so affected all of mankind.

Genesis 20:18

When Abraham went to Gerar, among the Philistines, and misrepresented his wife, *¹⁸The*

LORD *had closed up all the wombs of the house of Abimelech because of Sarah, Abraham's wife.*

Deuteronomy 7:12–14

For Israel, God promised blessing for obedience: [12]Then it shall come to pass, because you listen to these judgments, and keep and do them, that the LORD your God will keep with you the covenant and the mercy which He swore to your fathers: [13]And He will love you and bless you and multiply you; He will also bless the fruit of your womb... [14]You shall be blessed above all peoples; there shall not be a male or female barren among you or among your livestock. (See also 28:4, 11, 18.)

Psalm 37:38

The future of the wicked shall be cut off.

Psalm 128:1, 3, 6

[1]Blessed is every one who fears the LORD, Who walks in His ways.... [3]Your wife shall be like a fruitful vine In the very heart of your house, Your children like olive plants All around your table.... [6]Yes, may you see your children's children. Peace be upon Israel!

3. God is able to give children even when the physical conditions would make pregnancy and childbirth impossible. God can do miracles.

Genesis 17:15–19, 21; 18:10–14

God promised that Sarah would bear a son when she was ninety and Abraham an hundred years old (17:17), and after Sarah had passed menopause (18:11). See also Hebrews 11:11–12.

Luke 1:13–25, 36, 57

Zacharias and Elisabeth had had no children (vv. 7, 25) and this lack was considered a reproach to her. Now, when they were both well stricken in years, and Zacharias called himself an old man (vv. 7, 18), God promised a son, saying, *[13]...Do not be afraid, Zacharias, for your prayer is heard; and your wife Elizabeth will bear you a son, and you shall call his name John. [14]And you will have joy and gladness, and many will rejoice at his birth.... [24]Now after those days his wife Elizabeth conceived.... [57]...she brought forth a son.*

Luke 1:31–38

Mary had a hard time believing that she would have a son, since she was a virgin. She asked, *[34]...How can this be, since I do not know a man? [35]And the angel answered and said to her, "The Holy Spirit will come upon you, and the power of the Highest will overshadow you; therefore, also, that Holy One who is to be born will be called the Son of God.... [37]For with God nothing will be impossible."*

Matthew 1:20–25

When Joseph was troubled about Mary's pregnancy, an angel appeared to him in a dream saying, *[20]...Joseph, son of David, do not be afraid to take to you Mary your wife, for that which is conceived in her is of the Holy Spirit.... [22]Now all this was done, that it might be fulfilled which was spoken by the Lord through the prophet, saying, [23]"Behold, a virgin shall be with child, and bear a Son...." [24]Then Joseph...took to him his wife: [25]And did not know her till she had brought forth her firstborn Son. And he called His name Jesus.*

> *"Of all the joys that brighten suffering earth, what joy is welcomed like a newborn child?"*
> —Caroline Norton (1808–1877), English writer.

4. God controls conception.

Genesis 20:17–18

[17]So Abraham prayed to God; and God healed Abimelech, his wife, and his maidservants. Then they bore children. [18]For the LORD had closed up all the wombs of the house of Abimelech because of Sarah, Abraham's wife.

Genesis 21:1–3

[1]And the LORD visited Sarah as He had said, and the LORD did for Sarah as He had spoken. [2]For Sarah conceived, and bore Abraham a son in his old age, at the set time of which God had spoken to him.

Genesis 25:21

Now Isaac pleaded with the LORD for his wife, because she was barren; and the LORD granted his plea, and Rebekah his wife conceived.

Genesis 29:31

When the LORD saw that Leah was unloved, He opened her womb; but Rachel was barren.

Genesis 30:2, 22–23

2And Jacob's anger was aroused against Rachel, and he said, "Am I in the place of God, who has withheld from you the fruit of the womb? ..." 22Then God remembered Rachel, and God listened to her and opened her womb. 23And she conceived, and bore a son, and said, "God has taken away my reproach."

Judges 13:2–3, 24

In the time of the judges in Israel, *2Now there was a certain man from Zorah, of the family of the Danites, whose name was Manoah; and his wife was barren and had no children. 3And the angel of the LORD appeared to the woman, and said to her, Indeed now, you are barren and have borne no children, but you shall conceive and bear a son.... 24So the woman bore a son and called his name Samson; and the child grew, and the LORD blessed him.*

1 Samuel 1:5–6, 19, 27; 2:21

5He [Elkanah] loved Hannah: although the LORD had closed her womb. 6And her rival also provoked her severely, to make her miserable, because the LORD had closed her womb.... 19Elkanah knew Hannah his wife, and the LORD remembered her.

Job 1:21

Job's testimony that it was the Lord who gave him children: *21...The LORD gave, and the LORD hath taken away; blessed be the name of the LORD.*

Psalm 107:38, 41

38He [the Lord] also blesses them, and they multiply greatly; And He does not let their cattle decrease.... 41Yet He sets the poor on high, far from affliction, And makes their families like a flock.

Psalm 113:9

He grants the barren woman a home, Like a joyful mother of children. Praise the LORD. (See also 128:1–3.)

Isaiah 45:10 (NASB)

Woe to him who says to a father, "What are you begetting?" or to a woman, "To what are you giving birth?"

5. Life begins at conception.

a. The fetus has individuality, and is known to God as a person.

Genesis 25:21–23

21Now Isaac pleaded with the LORD for his wife, because she was barren; and the LORD granted his plea, and Rebekah his wife conceived. 22But the children struggled together within her; and she said, "If all is well, why am I this way?" So she went to inquire of the LORD. 23And the LORD said to her: 'Two nations are in your womb, two peoples shall be separated from your body, one people shall be stronger than the other, and the older shall serve the younger."

Psalm 139:13, 15–16

13For You have formed my inward parts; You have covered me in my mother's womb.... 15My frame was not hidden from You, When I was made in secret, And skillfully wrought in the lowest parts of the earth. 16Your eyes saw my substance, being yet unformed. And in Your book they all were written, The days fashioned for me, When as yet there were none of them.

Isaiah 49:1, 5

1...The LORD has called me from the womb; from the matrix of My mother He has made mention of My name.... 5And now, the LORD says, who formed Me from the womb to be His Servant...

Jeremiah 1:4–5

4Then the word of the LORD came unto me, saying, 5Before I formed you in the womb I knew you; before you were born I sanctified you; and I ordained you a prophet to the nations.

Luke 1:41, 44

41And it happened, when Elizabeth heard the greeting of Mary, that the babe leaped in her womb; and Elizabeth was filled with the Holy Spirit. Elizabeth testified: 44"For, indeed, as soon as the voice of your greeting sounded in my ears, the babe leaped in my womb for joy."

Romans 9:10–13

A New Testament reference to the event of Genesis 25:21–23: *11(for the children not yet being born, nor having done any good or evil, that the purpose of God according to election might stand, not of works but of Him who calls) ¹²It was said to her, "The older shall serve the younger."*

b. Under the Law, causing a miscarriage was a punishable offense.

Exodus 21:22

If men fight, and hurt a woman with child, so that she gives birth prematurely, yet no lasting harm follows, he shall surely be punished accordingly as the woman's husband imposes on him; and he shall pay as the judges determine.

"Chastity enables the soul to breathe a pure air in the foulest places."
—Josepth Joubert (1754–1824), French moralist.

"No padlock, bolts, or bars can secure a maiden so well as her own reserve."
—Saavedra M. de Cervantes (1547–1616), Spanish writer.

"God has set the type of marriage everywhere throughout the creation...Every creature seeks its perfection in another...The very heavens and earth picture it to us."
—Martin Luther (1483–1546), Reformation leader.

"God sends children for another purpose than merely to keep up the race—to enlarge our hearts; and to make us unselfish and full of kindly sympathies and affections, to give our souls higher aims; to call out all our faculties to extended enterprise and exertion; and to bring round our firesides bright faces, happy smiles, and loving, tender hearts...My soul blesses the great Father, every day, that he has gladdened the earth with little children."
—Mary Howitt (1799–1888), English author.

TALKING ABOUT SEX WITH CHILDREN

1. *Teachers must be comfortable with their own sexual relationships.*
2. *Teachers must have a deep reverence for life, and see the passing on of life as a holy thing.*
3. *Teachers must know correct but non-technical terminology, and be open and honest in answering questions.*
4. *Teachers must have convictions on the difficult questions which will come sooner than expected. They must also be willing to refer some questions to parents or pastors.*
5. *Teachers must be sensitive to the real questions behind those that children ask.*
—Adapted from F. Margaret Clarkson, "How to Answer your Child's Questions about Sex," *Moody Monthly,* November, 1977.

Physical Education

[Fine Arts/Health]

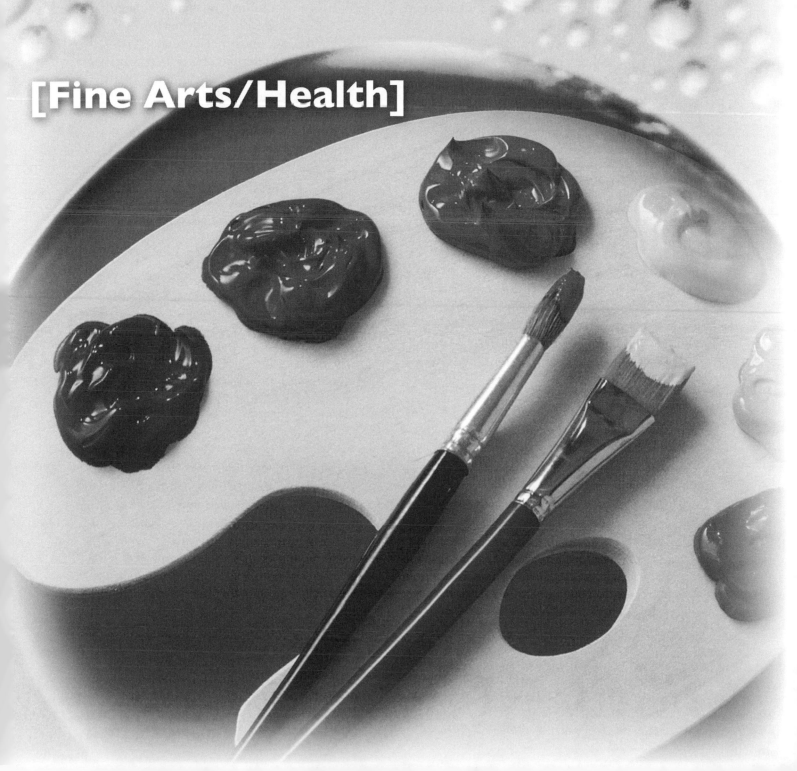

Physical Education: Biblical Concepts

1. The value of physical achievement and fitness is implied in Scripture.
2. Physical size and ability are of sufficient importance for God to have mentioned them in His Word.
   a. Men of unusual size are described.
   b. Men of great skill in archery, and in use of spear, sword, and sling as weapons are described.
   c. Men renowned for their speed in running are described.
   d. Men who performed unusual feats in old age are described.
3. Games and athletic competition provide many pictures of the Christian life.
   a. An adequate goal inspires the athlete.
   b. The race is a challenge to the runner who is fit.
   c. All contestants do not win equally.
   d. Self-discipline is essential for one who would win.
   e. Obedience to the rules of the game is required.
   f. Confidence in, and dependence on, the coach are crucial.
4. Play, in contrast to athletic competition, has the sense of celebration, or of complete freedom and enjoyment.
5. Certain physical activities are described as expressions of varied emotions.
   a. Dancing was common in Bible times, and was the "expression of joy by rhythmic movements of the limbs to musical accompaniment."
   b. Dancing had two major purposes: as the celebration of public victories or special occasions, and as an act of worship—the two often intertwined.
   c. Dancing in Bible times was done separately by men and women, with women the more frequent dancers.
   d. Dancing was at times used for evil purposes.
   e. Clapping is portrayed as an indication of either joy or contempt.
6. God sets standards for our activities that are distinct from those of the secular world.
   a. We must give priority to godly attitudes and living rather than to mere physical achievement.
   b. We must not be enticed by sinners or corrupted by evil companions.
   c. We must not be controlled by the desires of the flesh, by lust.
   d. We must avoid the appearance of evil, or that which would cause others to stumble.
   e. We must recognize the long-range effects of what we do now.
   f. We must be concerned for God's glory in all our choices.

"The world would have us believe that winning or success is measured by points on a scoreboard or by dollar signs. The Christian realizes that winning or success is determined by whether or not a goal has been achieved, and that goal is to bring glory to God."
—Thomas M. Boqdon, "A Christian View of Athletics," *Christian Home and School,* December, 1975, p. 20.

"Life is a series of games—games of finding answers, finding amusement, persuading people, winning friends, raising families and performing rituals. Some persons relish the game of life and enjoy all the subgames to the hilt. Others play them grimly, with their eyes fixed on the scoreboard, too much concerned with staying ahead to enjoy the game."
—Writer unknown; quoted in "Should Children Compete in Sports?" *The Christian Teacher,* November/December, 1975, p. 19.

Physical Education:
Biblical Background

> "Play was removed from the church after the Christian Middle Ages came to an end. Because the Church of Rome was using art as propaganda, the Protestants came to fear art and play. The influence of stoicism and neoplatonism worked further to destroy true play among the Protestant churches, though the Puritans were generally a joyous people. Luther's Table Talk is one of the last good examples of down–to–earth Christian fun and play."
>
> —James B. Jordan, "Play in Christian Perspective," *The Biblical Educator*, November, 1981.

Most of the health aspects of physical education are dealt with in Chapter 4, "Health." Concepts included here are those related especially to physical activity and achievement, recreational activities, and the believer's involvement in them.

1. The value of physical achievement and fitness is implied in Scripture.

Deuteronomy 34:7

The unusual strength and eyesight of Moses at 120 years of age is cited by God: *⁷Moses was one hundred and twenty years old when he died. His eyes were not dim nor his natural vigor abated.*

Joshua 14:10–12

Caleb was forty years old when he and Joshua with the other spies visited the land and Moses promised him an inheritance there. Now he is eighty–five and claims his inheritance from Joshua: *¹⁰...The Lord has kept me alive, as He said, these forty–five years...here I am this day, eighty–five years old. ¹¹As yet I am as strong this day as I was on the day that Moses sent me; just as my strength was then, so now is my strength for war, both for going out and for coming in. ¹²Now therefore give me this mountain...for you heard in that day how the Anakims [giants] were there, and that the cities were great and fortified. It may be that the Lord will*

be with me, and I shall be able to drive them out as the Lord said. Caleb's unusual physical stamina was worthy of recognition in God's Word.

Proverbs 31:17

The virtuous woman described in this chapter is one who *girds herself with strength, and strengthens her arms.* She is strong physically.

Isaiah 40:31

Of the comparisons made here, two refer to men's physical endurance as something positive. The emphasis is on spiritual strength that comes from waiting on the Lord, but only if the physical ability is of value is the figure of speech meaningful. *But those who wait on the Lord shall renew their strength; they shall mount up with wings like eagles, they shall run and not be weary, they shall walk and not faint.*

Galatians 2:2

Paul, in giving his testimony, tells of going to visit the apostles in Jerusalem fourteen years after his conversion. He says,...*Lest by any means I might run, or had run, in vain.* He uses the figure of running in a race, implying that such running is for some purpose, not something to be done in vain.

Philippians 2:16

Here again, Paul uses the same figure of speech, expressing concern that believers to whom he had ministered should exemplify their salvation in their lives (vv. 12–16). By so doing, there would be evidence that his work, described as a race, had not been in vain. Running is for a purpose! *¹⁶Holding fast the word of life, so that I may rejoice in the day of Christ that I have not run in vain or labored in vain.*

1 Timothy 4:8

For bodily exercise profits a little, but godliness is profitable for all things, having promise of the life that now is and of that which is to come.

2 Timothy 2:5

And also if anyone competes in athletics, he is not crowned unless he competes according to the rules.

Striving for athletic victory is presented as an honorable activity, one from which we should take a lesson.

2. Physical size and ability are of sufficient importance for God to have mentioned them in His Word.

a. Men of unusual size are described.

Numbers 13:28–33

The report of the spies: *²⁸Nevertheless the people who dwell in the land are strong; the cities are fortified and very large; moreover we saw the descendants of Anak there.... ³¹They are stronger than we. ³²...The land... is a land that devours—its inhabitants, and all the people whom we saw in it are men of great stature. ³³There we saw the giants [the descendants of Anak came from the giants]; and we were like grasshoppers in our own sight, and so we were in their sight.* See also Deuteronomy 1:28, where Moses recounts this incident to the new generation.

Deuteronomy 2:10–11, 19–21

Descriptions of areas through which Israel was to pass, along with some of the past history: *¹⁰The Emim had dwelt there* [i.e., in Ar on the border of Moab] *in times past, a people as great and numerous and tall as the Anakim. ¹¹They were also regarded as giants.... ¹⁹And when you come near the people of Ammon, do not harass them:... because I have given it to the descendants of Lot as a possession. ²⁰That was also regarded as a land of giants; giants formerly dwelt there.... ²¹A people as great and numerous and tall as the Anakim. But the* Lord *destroyed them before them.*

Deuteronomy 3:11

A description of Og, king of Bashan, over whom God had given victory: *¹⁴For only Og king of Bashan remained of the remnant of giants. Indeed his bedstead was an iron bedstead...nine cubits* [13½ feet] *is its length and four cubits* [6 feet] *its width, according to the standard cubit.*

Deuteronomy 9:1–3

Moses, on the day that Israel was to pass over Jordan, reminded them of the giants, and also of God's ability to give victory, in spite of the giants.

Joshua 11:21–22

When the conquest of Canaan was complete and the record of accomplishments made: *²²None of the Anakim were left in the land of the children of Israel; they remained only in Gaza, in Gath, and in Ashdod.*

Joshua 15:13–14 and Judges 1:20

When the land was divided, Caleb was given the city of Hebron where three sons of Anak, giants, still lived. Caleb drove them out.

1 Samuel 9:2

When Saul was chosen to be the first king of Israel, he was described as a choice young man, and goodly: *There was not a more handsome person than he among the children of Israel. From his shoulders upward he was taller than any of the people.* (See also 10:23.)

1 Samuel 17:4–7

Goliath described: height, over 9 feet; his bronze coat of mail weighing 200 pounds; the head of his iron spear weighing 25 pounds. (Weights taken from *The Berkeley Version in Modern English*, Zondervan, 1959.)

2 Samuel 21:19–20 and 1 Chronicles 20:4–8

Giants from among the Philistines and related to Goliath are described. They were killed by David and his servants, about 25 years after Goliath's death.

PROJECT: Unusual Strength. Study Judges 14–16 for the account of Samson. Pick out the demonstrations of strength and of weakness in his life. Consider more than the physical aspects.

---

b. Men of great skill in archery, and in the use of spear, sword, and sling as weapons are described.

Judges 20:16

A select band of warriors of the tribe of Benjamin is described: *¹⁶Among all this people there were seven hundred select men who were left–handed; every one could sling a stone at a hair's breadth and not miss.*

1 Samuel 17:34–37
David testifies to his skill and the Lord's deliverance from a lion and a bear, and his killing of both.

1 Samuel 17:40, 49–50
David's action in killing Goliath showed not only confidence in the Lord, but also great skill in the use of the sling.

1 Samuel 20:20–22, 35–38
Jonathan had skill in the use of the bow and arrow. He could place the arrow where he wanted it.

1 Chronicles 11:11
Jashobeam, one of David's mighty men, chief of the captains, killed 300 Philistines at one time with a spear.

1 Chronicles 11:22–23
Benaiah, another of David's mighty men, killed two lionlike men of Moab, a lion, and an Egyptian giant seven and a half feet tall.

1 Chronicles 12:1–7
A group of ambidextrous men gathered around David of Ziklag, when he was fleeing from Saul. *2Armed with bows, using both the right hand and the left in hurling stones and shooting arrows with the bow...* These were from the tribe of Benjamin.

1 Chronicles 12:8
A band of Gadites also gathered around David in the desert. They are described as *men of mighty men of valor, men trained for battle, who could handle shield and spear, whose faces were like the faces of lions, and were as swift as gazelles on the mountains.*

c. Men renowned for their speed in running are described.

2 Samuel 1:23
Saul and Jonathan are described as *swifter than eagles, they were stronger than lions.*

2 Samuel 2:18
Asahel was as *fleet of foot as a wild gazelle.*

2 Samuel 18:23–27
Ahimaaz was recognized by David's watchman by his running.

1 Kings 18:46
After the contest on Mount Carmel, when the rainstorm came, Ahab rode to Jezreel, but the *hand of the LORD came upon Elijah; and he girded up his loins and ran ahead of Ahab to the entrance of Jezreel.*

1 Chronicles 12:8
The band of men from Gad who followed David were not only well-trained in the use of shield and spear, but they were *as swift as gazelles on the mountains.*

Also the following passages tell of large numbers of runners whose responsibility it was to run before the chariots of kings and princes: 1 Samuel 8:11; 2 Samuel 15:1; 1 Kings 1:5.

d. Men who performed unusual feats in old age are described.

Deuteronomy 34:7 (quoted earlier)
The remarkable physical abilities of Moses at 120 years.

Joshua 14:10–12 (quoted earlier)
Caleb's eagerness to tackle the capture of Hebron at age eighty-five, in spite of giants in the land.

NOTE: In all of the above records, the significant fact is not merely that these men showed unusual skill or achievement of some kind, but that, in a Book written primarily to tell of God and His workings, and to show men how they may have eternal life in Christ, such details should be recorded for our enlightenment.

"Certainly work is not always required of a man. There is such a thing as a sacred idleness—the cultivation of which is now fearfully neglected."
—George Macdonald (1804–1905), Scottish novelist.

3. Games and athletic competition provide many pictures of the Christian life.

a. An adequate goal inspires the athlete.

1 Corinthians 9:24–27

24Do you not know that those who run in a race all run, but one receives the prize? Run in such a way that you may obtain it. 25And everyone who competes for the prize is temperate in all things. Now they do it to obtain a perishable crown, but we for an imperishable crown. 26Therefore I run thus: not with uncertainty. Thus I fight: not as one who beats the air: 27But I discipline my body and bring it into subjection, lest, when I have preached to others, I myself should become disqualified. [i.e., disapproved]. Note here the emphasis on the prize, the crown, obtaining, not being disqualified.

1 Corinthians 15:32

Paul here stresses the futility of the Christian life if there is no future, no resurrection of the dead. *32If, in the manner of men, I have fought with beasts at Ephesus, what advantage is it to me? If the dead do not rise, "Let us eat and drink, for tomorrow we die."* The figure of speech here refers to the gladiatorial games in which men fought with wild beasts.

Galatians 2:2 and Philippians 2:16

In each of these verses, Paul expresses concern that he not run in vain, or for no purpose or goal.

Philippians 3:12–14

12Not that I have already attained, or am already perfected; but I press on, that I may lay hold of that for which Christ Jesus has also laid hold of me. 13Brethren, I do not count myself to have apprehended; but one thing I do, forgetting those things which are behind and reaching forward to those things which are ahead, 14I press toward the goal for the prize of the upward call of God in Christ Jesus.

2 Timothy 4:7–8

7I have fought a good fight, I have finished the race, I have kept the faith: 8Finally, there is laid up for me the crown of righteousness, which the Lord, the righteous Judge, will give to me on that Day, and not to me only but also to all who have loved His appearing.

b. The race is a challenge to the runner who is fit.

Psalm 19:5

Here, the sunrise is likened to a strong man eager to begin his race. The race is no drudgery to him; it is what he has trained for.

Isaiah 40:28–31

Here, those who are spiritually fit are promised exhilaration in the running of the race of life. *29He [The Lord] gives power to the weak, and to those who have no might He increases strength. 30Even the youths shall faint and be weary, and the young men shall utterly fall: 31But those who wait on the LORD shall renew their strength; they shall mount up with wings like eagles, they shall run and not be weary, they shall walk and not faint.*

c. All contestants do not win equally.

1 Corinthians 9:24 (quoted previously)

Note here that though Paul reminds the reader that in a race this is true, he also exhorts believers that they should so run that they may obtain.

Hebrews 12:1 and Hebrews 11

Hebrews 11 portrays a variety of believers who trusted God and won the race of life. The results were not the same in any two lives; neither were the experiences; God, however, testifies to their winning, and describes them as a cloud of witnesses whose lives demonstrate the worthwhileness of the race.

d. Self–discipline is essential for one who would win.

1 Corinthians 9:25, 27 (quoted previously)

Note these expressions: *Is temperate in all things* [v. 25]... *I discipline my body, and bring it into subjection* [v. 27].

Philippians 3:13–14 (quoted previously)

Note especially: *Forgetting those things which are behind, and reaching forward...I press toward the goal...*

2 Timothy 4:7 (quoted previously)

Paul said he was persistent; he finished the race.

Hebrews 12:1–2

1Therefore we also, since we are surrounded by so great a cloud of witnesses, let us lay aside every *weight, and the sin which so easily ensnares us, and let us run with endurance the race that is set before us, ²Looking unto Jesus the author and finisher of our faith...*The writer here stresses the necessity of putting aside anything which would hinder in the race, whether something actually sinful, or merely something which slows one down and hinders progress. He also emphasizes patience in the race. Progress in the Christian life, as in athletics, does not come suddenly and without effort.

e. Obedience to the rules of the game is required.

1 Corinthians 9:27 (quoted earlier)

Paul expresses concern that he keep himself under control, lest when he had preached to others he should be disqualified or disapproved. The context makes clear that Paul is speaking of rewards for service, not salvation. The prize is something to be earned through faithful service; salvation is a gift given to those who trust Christ.

2 Timothy 2:5

And also if anyone competes in athletics, he is not crowned unless he competes according to the rules.

2 Timothy 4:8 (quoted previously)

Because Paul knows that he has fought a good fight and finished the course, he is confident that the crown will be his.

f. Confidence in, and dependence on, the coach are crucial.

Hebrews 12:2 (quoted previously)

Two reasons are given for looking unto Jesus: (1) He is *the author and finisher of our faith,* i.e., He is both the originator or leader of it, and He is also the perfecter of it. (2) In addition, He is the example for us. He saw the goal, He ignored the bystanders and endured the cross, He won God's approval.

Special Note: Because of the foregoing Christian life principles found in sports activities, the Christian school, it seems, should make use of athletics to develop Christian character. Various activities and contests may be looked at as roleplay of the Christian life. Important traits include the following:

—willingness to sacrifice for a long–range goal
—consideration for others
—ability to accept criticism and profit by it
—teamwork
—ability to lose gracefully
—determination, persistence, self–discipline
—obedience to rules and to directions from the one in charge

4. Play, in contrast to athletic competition, has the sense of celebration, or of complete freedom and enjoyment.

Several Hebrew words are translated play in the *King James Version.* Of those not referring to the playing of a musical instrument, one word is most common and appears in two kinds of contexts: (1) celebration and (2) leisurely, sporting activity.

1 Samuel 18:7

After David's victory over Goliath: *⁷So the women sang as they danced, and said: "Saul has slain his thousands, and David his ten thousands."* In the *New American Standard Bible,* the marginal reading is dancing, with the sense of celebration.

2 Samuel 6:5, 21 and 1 Chronicles 13:8

In these verses, describing David's activity before the Lord on the occasion of the bringing back the Ark on the cart, the word *play* is consistently used in the KJV, while the word *celebrate* is used in NASB.

1 Chronicles 15:29

Here when David was expressing his joy over the return of the Ark upon the shoulders of the Levites, his wife Michal, *looking through a window, saw King David whirling and playing music* (NKJV). The NASB substitutes the words, *leaping and making merry,* again the thought of celebration.

In addition to these uses indicating celebration, the same word is used in several places to convey the thought of fun, purposeless activity, making sport, or pure enjoyment:

Job 40:15–24

God in describing to Job behemoth, (15–24), a monstrous animal, so great that he is called *the first of the ways of God,* says his food comes from the mountains, *where all the beasts of the field play.*

Job 41:5

The Lord here speaks of leviathan, a great sea monster, asking Job, *⁵Will you play with him as with a bird?*

Psalm 104:26

The Psalmist speaks of the sea as the place where there is that *Leviathan Which You* [i.e., God] *have made to play therein.*

Proverbs 8:30–31 (NASB)

Wisdom personified is speaking here and is believed to represent the eternal Son of God. (See Scofield note.) This interpretation agrees with such passages as John 1:1–3 and Colossians 1:17. *³⁰Then I was beside Him, as a master craftsman, and I was daily; His delight, rejoicing, ³¹Rejoicing in His inhabited world, and my delight was with the sons of men.* The marginal reading for the word translated rejoicing, is playing, and the Hebrew word is the same as in the verses previously considered, and translated elsewhere as play.

James B. Jordan points out that here is Wisdom, the preincarnate Christ speaking, linking work and play before the throne of God. Therefore, he says, *"The play of Christians is an analogical replica of the play of the Son of God. It is sheer fun and delight in creation."* ("The Biblical Philosophy of Play" in the *Biblical Educator,* Nov., 1981.)

Zechariah 8:5

In the Kingdom, with Jesus present, happy children will play in the streets. *³Thus saith the LORD, I am returned unto Zion, and will dwell in the midst of Jerusalem.... ⁵And the streets of the city shall be full of boys and girls playing in the streets thereof.*

NOTE: In 2 Samuel 2:14, though the same word as in the previous passages is used and translated *play* in the KJV, the context clearly shows that much more was involved here, namely deadly combat. NASB translates the word here as *hold a contest,* and in the margin indicates that the literal meaning is *to make sport.*

5. **Certain physical activities are described as expressions of varied emotions.**

a. Dancing was common in Bible times, and was the "expression of joy by rhythmic movements of the limbs to musical accompaniment."

   (International Standard Bible Encyclopedia, 1947 Edition, p. 1169.)

Judges 11:34

Jephthah's daughter and her friends came dancing to meet her father on his safe return from a battle in which there had been victory.

Job 21:11–12

Job, describing the prosperity of the wicked says, *¹¹Their children dance. ¹²They sing to the tambourine and harp, and rejoice to the sound of the flute.*

Ecclesiastes 3:4

Solomon speaks of there being *⁴A time to weep, and a time to laugh; a time to mourn, and a time to dance.*

Lamentations 5:15

Jeremiah and God express their sorrow of heart because of Israel's sin and the resultant chastening: *¹⁵The joy of our heart has ceased, our dance has turned into mourning.* In other words, dancing and mourning are incompatible.

Matthew 11:17

Jesus, in describing men's lack of responsiveness to God's messengers, likens the situation to one where the musicians play but no one responds by dancing. Here is an indication that on many occasions the normal response to music was dancing.

Luke 15:25

Music and dancing were part of the celebration of the prodigal's return.

b. Dancing had two major purposes: as the celebration of public victories or special occasions, and as an act of worship—the two often intertwined.

Exodus 15:20–21

After the Red Sea experience: *20Then Miriam the prophetess, the sister of Aaron, took the timbrel in her hand; and all the women went out after her with timbrels and with dances. 21And Miriam answered them, "Sing to the LORD, for He has triumphed gloriously! The horse and its rider He has thrown into the sea."*

Judges 21:19–21

19... In fact, there is a yearly feast of the LORD.... 21...the daughters of Shiloh come out to perform....

1 Samuel 18:6–7

6...When David was returning from the slaughter of the Philistine [Goliath] ... the women had come out of all the cities of Israel, singing and dancing, to meet King Saul, with tambourines, with joy, and with musical instruments. 7So the women sang as they danced, and said: "Saul has slain his thousands, and David his ten thousands." (See also 21:11; 29:5.)

1 Samuel 30:16

Here was a similar celebration of a military victory in the invasion and destruction of Ziklag by the Amalekites, one of Israel's enemies. In it there was eating and drinking and dancing.

2 Samuel 6:14–16, 21, 23; See also 1 Chronicles 15:29

14Then David danced before the LORD with all his might; and David was wearing a linen ephod. 15So David and all the house of Israel brought up the ark of the LORD with shouting, and with the sound of the trumpet. 16...Michal...saw king David leaping and whirling before the LORD, and she despised him in her heart. David explained: *21...It was before the LORD, who chose me instead of your father and all his house...Therefore I will play music before the LORD.... 23Therefore Michal the daughter of Saul had no child to the day of her death.* [God apparently accepted David's actions.]

Psalm 30:11

The Psalmist's testimony, spoken in praise to the Lord: *11You have turned for me my mourning into dancing, You have put off my sackcloth and clothed me with gladness.*

Psalm 149:3

Let them [Israel] praise His name with the

dance; Let them sing praises to Him with the timbrel and harp.

Psalm 150:4

Praise Him with the timbrel and dance; Praise Him with stringed instruments and flutes.

Jeremiah 31:4, 13

God promises that in the days of the Kingdom, He will restore Israel and there will be great rejoicing: *4...You shall again be adorned with your tambourines, and shall go forth in the dances of those who rejoice.... 13 Then shall the virgin rejoice in the dance, and the young men and the old, together; for I will turn their mourning to joy, will comfort them, and make them rejoice rather than sorrow.*

c. Dancing in Bible times was done separately by men and women, with women the more frequent dancers.

See Jeremiah 31:13, quoted above.

PROJECT: Look up all the Bible references to dancing, using a good concordance to locate them. Make a chart with columns as follows: Reference, Occasion, Who danced, Comments. Summarize your findings, and contrast with modern dancing, both as to purpose and conduct of the dancing.

---

d. Dancing was at times used for evil purposes.

Exodus 32:19

Here, God's people danced in nakedness around the golden calf proclaiming it as their god.

1 Kings 18:26–29

On Mount Carmel, in the contest with Elijah, the prophets of Baal seem to have performed physical movements as well as praying to their god for action.

Matthew 14:6–8 and Mark 6:22

Herodias danced before Herod and so pleased him that he offered her anything she wanted, but this was part of a plot to kill John the Baptist. Her mother had instructed her previously to ask for John's head, and so she did.

e. Clapping is portrayed as an indication of either joy or contempt.

Note also that "Clap is used figuratively to denote 'Nature's sympathy' with God's people." (*International Standard Bible Encyclopedia*, 1947 Edition, p. 665.)

Examples of joy:

2 Kings 11:12

At the coronation of young King Joash after six years under the wicked Queen Athaliah, the priest Jehoida: *12...And he brought out the king's son, put the crown on him, and gave him the Testimony, they made him king and anointed him, and they clapped their hands and said, "Long live the king!"*

Psalm 47:1

O clap your hands, all you people; shout unto God with the voice of triumph.

Psalm 98:8–9

The Psalmist calls on everybody and everything to rejoice before the Lord. Among other specific exhortations, he says: *8Let the rivers clap their hands...Before the Lord.*

Isaiah 55:12

Here is a picture of the rejoicing to take place when Jesus Christ is king: *12... The mountains and the hills shall break forth into singing before you, and all the trees of the field shall clap their hands.*

Ezekiel 25:6

God promises judgment to the Ammonites because they rejoiced at the wrong things: *6...Because you clapped your hands, stamped your feet, and rejoiced in heart with all your disdain for the land of Israel.*

Examples of contempt or repudiation:

Job 27:23

Job speaking: *23Men shall clap their hands at him* [i.e., at the wicked], *and shall hiss him out of his place.*

Job 34:36–37

Elihu condemning Job: *36Oh, that Job were tried to the utmost... 37For he adds rebellion to his sin; he claps his hands among us, and multiplies his words against God.*

Lamentations 2:15

A description of reactions of passersby as they see Jerusalem broken down: *15All who pass by clap their hands at you; they hiss and shake their heads at the daughter of Jerusalem: "Is this the city that is called 'the perfection of beauty, the joy of the whole earth?'"*

Nahum 3:19

God's judgment pronounced on Nineveh: *19Your injury has no healing, your wound is severe. All who hear news of you will clap their hands over you.*

---

6. **God sets standards for our activities that are distinct from those of the secular world.**

---

a. We must give priority to godly attitudes and living rather than to mere physical achievement.

Psalm 147:10–11

Physical achievement has little significance to the Lord. *10He [God] does not delight in the strength of the horse; He takes no pleasure in the legs of a man. 11The Lord takes pleasure in those who fear Him, In those who hope in His mercy.*

Romans 13:14

But put ye on the Lord Jesus Christ, and make no provision for the flesh, to fulfill its lusts.

Philippians 4:8

Finally, brethren, whatever things are true, whatever things are noble, whatever things are just, whatever things are pure, whatever things are lovely, whatever things are of good report, if there is any virtue and if there is anything praiseworthy —meditate on these things.

Colossians 3:2

Set your mind on things above, not on things on the earth.

1 Timothy 4:8

For bodily exercise profits a little [or, for a little]: *but godliness is profitable for all things, having promise of the life that now is and of that which is to come.*

b. We must not be enticed by sinners or corrupted by evil companions.

Proverbs 1:10–15

¹⁰My son, if sinners entice you, do not consent. ¹¹If they say, "Come with us..." ¹³We shall find all kinds of precious possessions, we shall fill our houses with spoil: ¹⁴Cast in your lot among us, Let us all have one purse: ¹⁵My son, do not walk in the way with them, keep your foot from their path.

1 Corinthians 15:33 (NASB)

Do not be deceived. "Bad company corrupts good morals."

Ephesians 5:6–7

⁶Let no one deceive you with empty words, for because of these things the wrath of God comes upon the sons of disobedience. ⁷Therefore do not be partakers with them. ⁸For you were once darkness, but now you are light in the Lord. Walk as children of light.

James 4:4

Adulterers and adulteresses! Do you not know that friendship with the world is enmity with God? Whoever therefore wants to be a friend of the world makes himself an enemy of God.

c. We must not be controlled by the desires of the flesh, by lust.

Proverbs 4:23, 25–27

²³Keep your heart with all diligence, for out of it spring the issues of life.... ²⁵Let your eyes look straight ahead, and your eyelids look right before you. ²⁶Ponder the path of your feet, and let all your ways be established. ²⁷Do not turn to the right or the left; remove your foot from evil.

1 John 2:15–17

¹⁵Do not love the world or the things in the world. If anyone loves the world, the love of the Father is not in him. ¹⁶For all that is in the world—the lust of the flesh, the lust of the eyes, and the pride of life—is not of the Father but is of the world. ¹⁷And the world is passing away, and the lust of it; but he who does the will of God abides forever.

d. We must avoid the appearance of evil, or that which would cause others to stumble.

1 Corinthians 8:9, 12

⁹But beware lest somehow this liberty of yours become a stumbling block to those who are weak.... ¹²But when you thus sin against the brethren, and wound their weak conscience, you sin against Christ. (See also 10:32–33.)

2 Corinthians 6:3–4

We are to be those who ³give no offense in anything, that our ministry may not be blamed. ⁴But in all things we commend ourselves as ministers of God....

1 Thessalonians 5:22

Abstain from every form of evil.

e. We must recognize the long–range effects of what we do now.

Galatians 6:7–9

⁷Do not be deceived, God is not mocked, for whatever a man sows, that he will also reap. ⁸For he who sows to his flesh will of the flesh reap corruption, but he who sows to the Spirit will of the Spirit reap everlasting life. ⁹And let us not grow weary while doing good, for in due season we shall reap if we do not lose heart.

f. We must be concerned for God's glory in all our choices.

1 Corinthians 10:31

Therefore, whether you eat or drink, or whatever you do, do all to the glory of God.

Colossians 3:17

And whatever you do in word or deed, do all in the name of the Lord Jesus, giving thanks to God the Father through Him.

> *"God has His best things for the few that dare to stand the test; God has His second choice for those who will not have His best."*
> —A. B. Simpson.

Death Education

[Fine Arts/Health]

Death Education: Biblical Concepts

I. THE NATURE OF PHYSICAL DEATH

1. Death is the separation of the soul and spirit from the body.
2. Death means leaving all material things behind.
3. Death is universal, except as God intervenes.
4. Death results in the return of the body to dust.
5. Death for the believer means being in the immediate presence of the Lord; for the unbeliever, it means being in a place of torment.
6. Death, though sometimes called sleep, involves a continuation of consciousness.
   a. Death is spoken of as sleep, based on the appearance of the body.
   b. Death involves only the physical body, not the consciousness; people are fully conscious after death.
7. The nature of death as portrayed in the Old Testament is greatly amplified in the teachings of Christ and in His death and resurrection.

II. SPIRITUAL AND ETERNAL DEATH

1. Spiritual death is the separation of the soul from God; it is the condition of one who is alive physically, but who does not trust Christ as Savior and Lord.
2. Eternal death, or the second death, is the eternal banishment of the soul from God and heaven, and consignment to everlasting punishment; it results from continuance in spiritual death until physical death comes.

III. THE CAUSES OF DEATH

1. All death is ultimately the result of sin in the race—Adam's sin.
2. Death may be the result of God's judgment for sin, either committed by oneself or another.
3. Death may be commanded by God to be executed by man as part of his governmental responsibility.
4. Death may come about purely by the breakdown of the human body, whether by war, violence, accident, suicide or illness.

IV. THE DISPOSITION OF THE BODY

1. Burial is the most common Scriptural method for the disposition of the body.
   a. Burial is mentioned many times in the Bible, in both Old and New Testaments.
   b. Not to be buried is represented as a disgrace.
   c. Burials were often attended by friends and relatives.
   d. Many types of burying places are mentioned.
2. Cremation, wherever used in Scripture, is associated with those who have sinned flagrantly, or who have in some way disgraced God's people.
3. The use of spices, incense, and special garments or wrappings was often included in the preparation for burial.

V. LIFE AFTER DEATH

1. The immaterial part of man, the soul and spirit, continues to live after the body dies.
   a. Physical death is not the end; life continues.
   b. The kind of life we live after death, both immediately and later, depends on our responses to God's provision in this life.
   c. For the believer, the soul and spirit go immediately to be with Christ, an experience better than life on earth.
   d. For the unbeliever, the soul and spirit go immediately to a place of imprisonment and torment, with full consciousness.

e. Children who die before they knowingly sin go to be with the Lord.

2. The material part of every man, the physical body, will be resurrected and joined to the soul and spirit at a future time not known to man.

   a. Believers whose bodies have died will receive resurrection bodies when Christ comes to take all who have eternal life to be with Him—at the Rapture of the Church.

   b. Believers who have trusted Christ during the Great Tribulation, after the Rapture, and who have been martyred for their faith, will be raised at the end of the Tribulation and before the millennial reign begins.

   c. The resurrection bodies of believers will be recognizable, made of flesh and bones, yet changed and freed from limitations common to men today.

   d. The bodies of unbelievers will be raised 1000 years after the Tribulation saints, at the end of the thousand-year reign of Christ on earth.

   e. Unbelievers, after their resurrection, will appear at the Great White Throne, will be judged according to their works, and then cast into the lake of fire forever.

VI. POST-RESURRECTION EVENTS FOR BELIEVERS

1. Believers, in their new bodies, along with those living at the time and now changed, will be caught up together in the clouds, to meet the Lord in the air, and then be forever with Him in bodily form.

2. Believers will join in celebration of the culmination of their union with Christ, in the Marriage Supper of the Lamb.

3. Believers will appear before the judgment seat of Christ to be judged for their lives and service and for the presentation of rewards.

4. Believers will be identified with Christ as He reveals Himself to the world and establishes His millennial kingdom on earth.

5. Believers will participate in the new heaven and new earth, free from limitations due to sin, in a special place prepared by the Lord for His own.

VII. GOD'S POWER OVER DEATH

1. God's authority over death has been demonstrated on many occasions both independendtly and through His servants.

   a. The Bible records many instances of God's use of death as judgment for sin.

   b. The Bible records many occasions when, through the power of God, someone was raised from the dead.

2. God's power over death, as demonstrated in the resurrection of Christ, is presented as the basis for our faith.

VIII. THE BELIEVER'S ATTITUDE TOWARD PHYSICAL LIFE AND DEATH

1. Life is short; we must use it wisely.

2. Life is dependent on God—for its enablement and for its length.

   a. For its enablement

   b. For its length

3. The closing of life sometimes brings insights of special significance.

4. Death is not to be feared by believers, though it is rightfully feared by those who are not trusting the Savior.

   a. No fear for believers

   b. Rightful fear for unbelievers

5. The death of His saints is precious to the Lord.

6. Doing God's will day by day is more important than whether we live or die.

Death Education: Biblical Background

I. THE NATURE OF PHYSICAL DEATH

1. Death is the separation of the soul and spirit from the body.

Psalm 49:15

But God will redeem my soul from the power of the grave [sheol]; *for He shall receive me.*

Ecclesiastes 12:7

Verses 1–6 include a plea to make use of the days of youth in the light of old age and death which are sure to come. Part of that plea is a description of old age, and then of death: *⁷Then the dust will return to the earth as it was, and the spirit will return to God who gave it.*

James 2:26

For as the body without the spirit is dead, so faith without works is dead also.

2. Death means leaving all material things behind.

Psalm 49:16–17

¹⁶Do not be afraid when one becomes rich, When the glory of his house is increased; ¹⁷For when he dies he shall carry nothing away, His glory shall not descend after him. (See also v. 10.)

1 Timothy 6:7

For we brought nothing into this world, and it is certain we can carry nothing out.

See also Ecclesiastes 5:15.

3. Death is universal, except as God intervenes.

Psalm 49:6–12

⁶Those who trust in their wealth And boast in the multitude of their riches; ⁷None of them can by any means redeem his brother, nor give to God a ransom for him: ⁸For the redemption of their souls is costly, And it shall cease forever. ⁹That he should continue to live eternally, And not see the Pit. ¹⁰For he sees that wise men die; Likewise the fool and the

senseless person perish. And leave their wealth to others. *¹¹Their inward thought is, that their houses will continue forever, And their dwelling places to all generations; They call their lands after their own names. ¹²Nevertheless man, though in honor, does not remain; He is like the beasts that perish.* (See also 89:48.)

Amos 9:10

All the sinners of My people shall die by the sword, who say, "The calamity shall not overtake us nor confront us." In other words, though people think they will be the exception, their hope is not fulfilled.

Luke 12:20

Jesus speaking the parable of the rich fool who thought he could go on forever: *²⁰"But God said to him, 'You fool! This night your soul will be required of you; then whose will those things be which you have provided?' "*

Note also that when Seth had a son, he named him Enos, which means mortal. He recognized the universality of death, even though Adam was still living, and the only death he knew about was Abel's (Genesis 4:26). God does intervene however!

Genesis 5:24; Hebrews 11:5

²⁴And Enoch walked with God; and he was not, for God took him. [See also Hebrews 11:5.] *By faith Enoch was translated so that he did not see death, "and was not found because God had translated him"; for before his translation he had this testimony, that he pleased God.*

> *"Living is death; dying is life...On this side of the grave we are exiles, on that, citizens; on this side, orphans; on that, children; on this side, captives; on that, freemen; on this side disguised, unknown; on that, disclosed and proclaimed as the sons of God."*
> —Henry Ward Beecher.

2 Kings 2:11–12, 17

¹¹That suddenly a chariot of fire appeared with horses of fire, and separated the two of them; and Elijah went up by a whirlwind into heaven. ¹²Now Elisha saw it, and he cried out, "My father, my father, the chariot of Israel and its horsemen!" So he saw him no more... *17Therefore they sent fifty men, and they searched for three days but did not find him.*

John 14:3

Jesus speaking: *3And if I go and prepare a place for you, I will come again, and receive you to Myself; that where I am, there you may be also.*

Acts 1:9

Now when He [Jesus] had spoken these things, while they watched, He was taken up, and a cloud received Him out of their sight.

1 Corinthians 15:51–53

51Behold, I tell you a mystery: We shall not all sleep [died], but we shall all be changed, 52In a moment, in the twinkling of an eye, at the last trump. For the trumpet will sound, and the dead will be raised incorruptible, and we shall be changed. 53For this corruptible [i.e., dead body decaying] must put on incorruption, and this mortal [living person, subject to death] must put on immortality.

1 Thessalonians 4:16–17

16For the Lord Himself will descend from heaven with a shout, with the voice of an archangel, and with the trumpet of God. And the dead in Christ will rise first. 17Then we who are alive and remain shall be caught up together with them in the clouds to meet the Lord in the air. And thus we shall always be with the Lord.

4. Death results in the return of the body to dust.

Genesis 3:19

God's statement to Adam after the Fall: *19In the sweat of your face you shall eat bread till you return to the ground, for out of it you were taken; for dust you are, and to dust you shall return.*

Job 21:23–26

Job describes the different conditions of people at their death and concludes about all men: *26They lie down alike in the dust, and worms cover them.*

Job 24:19–20

19As drought and heat consume the snow

waters, so should the grave those who have sinned. *20The womb should forget him, the worm should feed sweetly on him...*

Psalm 49:6–10 (previously quoted)

Note, in verse 1, the recognition of corruption or decay of the body for all, rich and poor alike. See also in verse 14: *death shall feed on them...their beauty shall be consumed in the grave....*

Psalm 104:29

Referring to men and animals and their relationship to God: *29...You take away their breath, they die and return to their dust.* (See also Ecclesiastes 12:7, quoted previously).

5. Death for the believer means being in the immediate presence of the Lord; for the unbeliever, it means being in a place of torment.

Note: This concept will be dealt with more fully in a later section, entitled "Life after Death."

Luke 16:19–31

Here, in the description of the rich man and Lazarus, Lazarus is in "Abraham's bosom," while the rich man is in a place of torment. Each went to his respective place immediately upon death. Later, at the ascension of Christ, Abraham's bosom (or paradise) was moved to heaven (2 Cor. 12:1–4; Eph. 4:8–10). See *Scofield Bible* footnote for further explanation.

Luke 23:43

And Jesus [speaking to the thief on the cross] *said to him, "Assuredly, I say to you, today you will be with Me in Paradise."* He was to be immediately with the Lord.

2 Corinthians 5:8

Paul's testimony: *8We are confident, yes, well pleased rather to be absent from the body and to be present with the Lord.*

6. Death, though sometimes called sleep, involves a continuation of consciousness.

a. Death is spoken of as sleep, based on the appearance of the body.

Deuteronomy 31:16

God speaking to Moses: *Behold, you will rest with your fathers.* (See also Jeremiah 51:39.)

Job 7:21, 14:12

21For now I will lie down in the dust, and You will seek me diligently, but I will no longer be.... 12So man lies down and does not rise. Till the heavens are no more, they will not awake nor be roused from their sleep.

Daniel 12:2

And many of those who sleep in the dust of the earth shall awake, some to everlasting life, some to shame and everlasting contempt.

John 11:11–14

11[Jesus said], "Our friend Lazarus sleeps; but I go, that I may wake him up." 12His disciples said, "Lord, if he sleeps he will get well." 13However, Jesus spoke of his death, but they thought that He was speaking about taking rest in sleep. 14Then Jesus said to them plainly, "Lazarus is dead." Both Jesus and the disciples obviously knew the difference.

Acts 7:60

Stephen, when he was martyred, is said to have fallen asleep.

Acts 13:36

Paul, preaching in the synagogue, referred to David, saying, *36For David, after he had served his own generation by the will of God, fell asleep, was buried with his fathers, and saw corruption.* The reference is to the body, since it is that which decays.

1 Corinthians 11:30

Paul, referring to abuses of the Lord's Supper, said, *30For this cause many are weak and sickly among you, and many sleep.*

1 Corinthians 15:6, 18, 51

In this great resurrection chapter, Paul speaks of a great number of believers who were witnesses to the resurrected Lord and who are now fallen asleep; he further speaks of the futility of falling asleep in Christ if Christ did not rise bodily; he concludes by saying that *we shall not all sleep, but we shall all be changed.* Then follows an exclamation to Death, showing that it is limited to the body, and that therefore through the resurrection of Christ, the sting is gone.

1 Thessalonians 4:14–15

In describing the order of the Rapture, again the Apostle speaks of believers as *those who sleep in Jesus.*

b. Death involves only the physical body, not the consciousness; people are fully conscious after death.

Psalm 49:14–15

Speaking of those whose minds are centered on earthly things, the Psalmist describes their burial and decay; then in contrast he says, *15But God will redeem my soul from the power of the grave: for he shall receive me.* Here is expectation of being with the Lord, which means nothing unless one is conscious of where he is! (See also Psalm 23:6.)

Luke 16:19–31

The rich man and Lazarus: The rich man was conscious of his predicament, and of the imminent danger to his brothers, though they were not with him. He was also aware of Abraham and Lazarus and their more desirable situation. He was able to reason and argue. Abraham also was conscious; he knew about both men and their previous lives; he recognized the gulf between the areas of Hades; he remembered Moses and the prophets and the need for people to heed them; he also knew how contrary people are when it comes to believing God's message.

John 11:25

Jesus, speaking to Martha, explains that life does not end with death of the body. *25...I am the resurrection, and the life. He who believes in Me, though he may die, he shall live: 26And whoever lives and believes in Me shall never die. Do you believe this?*

John 11:43–44

Lazarus, though dead in body, responded to Jesus' command to come forth. Response demands consciousness.

Philippians 1:21, 23

Paul, though in prison at the time, considered his life in the body as the outliving of Christ; yet he said, *To die is gain.* He wanted to continue to minister to believers, but he also had a strong desire *to depart, and be with Christ; which,* he said, *is far better.* This preference on his part means little without the ability to enjoy the presence of the Lord.

Revelation 6:9–11; 7:9–10, 13–15

In each of these passages, martyrs are described as conscious, in one case asking, *How long?* and in the second case actively praising God. Not a picture of souls that are asleep!

---

7. The nature of death as portrayed in the Old Testament is greatly amplified in the teachings of Christ and in His death and resurrection.

For instance, in the Old Testament several passages portray death as the end, with no consciousness after death. This is not the universal portrayal, however, and neither is it a New Testament concept.

Job 14:12, 14

12So man lies down and does not rise. Till the heavens are no more, they will not awake nor be roused from their sleep.... 14If a man dies, shall he live again?

Job 17:13–16

13"If I wait, for the grave as my house, if I make my bed in the darkness. 14If I say to corruption, 'You are my father' and to the worm, 'You are my mother and my sister' 15Where then is my hope? As for my hope, who can see it? 16Will they go down to the gates of Sheol? Shall we have rest together in the dust."

Job 19:25–27 (NASB)

Here, in contrast, Job's expectation of life beyond the grave shines through: *25And as for me, I know that my Redeemer lives, And at the last He will take His stand on earth. 26Even after my skin is flayed* [or destroyed], *Yet without my flesh I shall see God; 27Whom I myself shall behold, And whom my eyes shall see and not another.*

Psalm 23:6

Here, David asserts his faith in life beyond the grave: *6...I will dwell in the house of the LORD forever.*

Ecclesiastes 9:5–6

5For the living know that they will die: but the dead know nothing, and they have no more reward, *for the memory of them is forgotten. 6Also their love, their hatred, and their envy have now perished; nevermore will they have a share in anything done under the sun.*

Isaiah 25:8

Here is one example out of many in the prophetic books in which life beyond death, in this case life in the Kingdom Age is described: *8He will swallow up death in forever, and the LORD God Will wipe away tears from all faces; the rebuke of His people He will take away from all the earth; for the LORD has spoken.*

It is of interest to note that when Job spoke his words describing the futility of life and the finality of death, he was under very severe attack by both Satan and his so-called friends. He was a discouraged man. Likewise, when Solomon wrote Ecclesiastes, he was an old man, who, in spite of special wisdom from the Lord, had let his riches and his many wives turn him to sin. Many of the concepts he expresses are those of a man away from God, a man reasoning only as a man. God records accurately man's thoughts.

II. SPIRITUAL AND ETERNAL DEATH

In addition to physical death, or death of the body, described in the previous section, the word death is used to refer to spiritual and eternal death. The distinctions are important to the understanding of Scripture.

---

1. Spiritual death is the separation of the soul from God; it is the condition of one who is alive physically, but who does not trust Christ as Savior and Lord.

John 5:24

Most assuredly, I say to you, he who hears My word and believes in Him who sent Me has everlasting life, and shall not come into judgment, but has passed from death into life.

Romans 7:11

Paul was obviously alive physically when he said: *11For sin, taking occasion by the commandment, deceived me, and by it killed me.*

Romans 8:6–8

⁶For to be carnally [fleshly] minded is death; but to be spiritually minded is life and peace. ⁷Because the carnal mind is enmity against God: for it is not subject to the law of God, nor indeed can be. (See also 24–25.)

Ephesians 2:1–5

¹And you He made alive who were dead in trespasses and sins. ⁵Even when we were dead in trespasses, made us alive together with Christ... (See also Colossians 2:13.)

1 Timothy 5:6

Paul speaking of ungodly widows: *⁶But who lives in pleasure is dead while she lives.*

1 John 5:12

He who has the Son has life; he who does not have the Son of God does not have life.

---

2. Eternal death, or the second death, is the eternal banishment of the soul from God and heaven, and consignment to everlasting punishment; it results from continuance in spiritual death until physical death comes.

John 8:21, 24

²¹Then Jesus said to them again, "I am going away, and you will seek Me, and will die in your sin. Where I go you cannot come.... ²⁴Therefore I said to you that you will die in your sins; for if you do not believe that I am He, you will die in your sins."

Revelation 2:11

He who has an ear, let him hear what the Spirit says to the churches. He who overcomes shall not be hurt by the second death. As long as there is physical life, there is the possibility of escaping eternal death by turning to Christ.

Revelation 21:7–8

⁷He who overcomes shall inherit all things, and I will be his God and he shall be My son. ⁸But the cowardly, unbelieving, abominable, murderers, sexually immoral, sorcerers, idolaters, and all liars shall have their part in the lake which burns with fire and brimstone, which is the second death.

See also Matthew 10:28; 2 Thessalonians 1:8–9; Revelation 20:14.

III. THE CAUSES OF DEATH

1. All death is ultimately the result of sin in the race—Adam's sin.

Genesis 2:16–17

God provided for man's needs, but limited him with respect to one tree, the tree of the knowledge of good and evil, saying: *¹⁷...You shall not eat, for in the day that you eat of it you shall surely die.*

Genesis 3:19

God spoke to Adam after his sin: *¹⁹In the sweat of your face you shall eat bread till you return to the ground, for out of it you were taken; for dust you are, and to dust you shall return.*

Romans 5:12

Therefore, just as through one man sin entered the world, and death through sin, and thus death spread to all men, because all sinned.

1 Corinthians 15:21–22

²¹For since by man came death, by man came also the resurrection of the dead. ²²For as in Adam all die, even so in Christ all shall be made alive.

---

2. Death may be the result of God's judgment for sin, either committed by oneself or another.

Examples:

Genesis 38:7

⁷But Er, Judah's firstborn, was wicked in the sight of the LORD, and the LORD killed him.

Genesis 38:9–10

Onan, Er's brother, deliberately spilled sperm cells on the ground, *lest he should give an heir to his brother. ¹⁰And the thing which he did displeased the Lord: therefore He slew him also.*

Exodus 9:24–25, 12:29–30

In delivering Israel from Egypt two plagues involved God's taking the lives of Egyptians because Pharaoh would not let God's people go. *⁹:²⁴So there was hail, and fire mingled with the hail, so very heavy... ²⁵And the hail struck throughout the whole land of Egypt, all that was in the field, both man and beast.*

¹²:²⁹[Passover] *And it came to pass, at midnight the LORD smote all the firstborn in the land of Egypt, from the firstborn of Pharaoh that sat on his throne unto the firstborn of the captive that was in the dungeon; and all the firstborn of cattle. ³⁰...There was not a house where there was not one dead.*

Exodus 30:17–21

God was very specific about the rules for worship in the tabernacle. He specified that they were to make a laver. *¹⁹For Aaron and his sons shall wash their hands and their feet in water from it: ²⁰When they go into the tabernacle of the meeting, or when they come near the altar to minister, to burn an offering made by fire to the LORD, they shall wash with water, lest they die;... ²¹And it shall be a statute forever to them....*

Exodus 30:37–38

Incense was to be compounded especially for use in the tabernacle, but similar incense was not to be used for other purposes. *³⁸Whoever makes any like it, to smell it, he shall be cut off from his people.*

Numbers 11:1

At Taberah, on the way from Egypt to Canaan, *Now when the people complained, it displeased the LORD; for the LORD heard it, and His anger was aroused. So the fire of the LORD burned among them, and consumed some....*

Numbers 11:33, 35

The Lord struck with a plague which killed many because of the dissatisfaction shown in their demand for meat.

Numbers 14:28–33

When the ten spies brought back the evil report from Canaan, and the people refused to enter the land, the Lord said: *²⁹The carcasses of you who have murmured against Me shall fall in this wilderness, all of you who were numbered, according to your entire number, from twenty years old and above. ³⁰...Except for Caleb...and Joshua... ³³And your sons shall be shepherds...forty years...until your carcasses are consumed in the wilderness.... ³⁷Those very men who brought the evil report about the land, died by the plague before the LORD* [i.e., they died immediately]. See also 26:64–65 for fulfillment.

Numbers 16:1–35

The earth swallowed up Korah, Dathan, and Abiram and their families for their refusal to accept the leadership God had appointed. Fire from God consumed 250 of their followers.

Numbers 16:41–50

The Lord sent a plague that killed 14,700 persons because Israel murmured and blamed Moses and Aaron for the deaths described above.

2 Samuel 12:15, 18

God was displeased with David for his adultery with Bathsheba and his arranging for the murder of Uriah. As a result, *¹⁵...And the LORD struck the child that Uriah's wife bore to David, and it became very ill... ¹⁸...the child died.*

1 Kings 14:7–11

God promised to judge every male of the house of Jeroboam because of Jeroboam's sins. None except one son would die a natural death and be buried (v. 13). 1 Kings 15:29–30 gives the fulfillment.

1 Kings 16:1–4 and 11–13

A similar judgment came to Baasha and his sons, for following Jeroboam's example.

2 Kings 1:3–4, 16–17

King Ahaziah of Israel, in time of illness following an accident, sent to inquire of Baalzebub rather than God. The Lord sent word by Elijah that because of this he would die.

See also 2 Kings 1:10–12; 2:23–24.

Acts 5:1–11

Ananias and Sapphira, in the newly formed Jerusalem church, lied about their contribution, and God took their lives.

1 Corinthians 11:29–30

In the Corinthian church there was much confusion; one kind of confusion and carelessness related to the observance of the Lord's Supper (vv. 20–22). Paul warned believers then and now that sickness and death may be the result of failure to consider seriously what that ordinance represents.

1 John 5:16–17

¹⁶If anyone sees his brother sinning a sin which does not lead to death, he will ask, and He will give him life for those who commit sin not leading to death. There is sin leading to death. I do not say that he should pray about that. 17All unrighteousness is sin: and there is sin not to death.

It should be noted that, while there are many more cases of God's judgment by death under the Law than are recorded in the New Testament, God has so judged in the church age, too.

3. Death may be commanded by God to be executed by man as part of his governmental responsibility.

Genesis 9:6

Whoever sheds man's blood, by man his blood shall be shed; for in the image of God He made man.

Exodus 35:2 and Numbers 15:32–36

The Sabbath was to be a sign between God and Israel; whoever did not keep it as a holy day was to be put to death.

Numbers 18:1–7, 22–23

Only the sons of Aaron and the Levites were to have responsibilities related to the tabernacle service; a stranger who intruded was to be put to death (v. 7); also an Israelite of another tribe was excluded on penalty of death (v. 22).

Numbers 25:4–5, 9

Israelites who joined themselves to Baal were put to death at the command of God through Moses.

Numbers 35:16–21, 29–34

The death penalty for murder instituted by God in Genesis 9, just after the Flood, was to be continued in Israel under the Law. God's reasoning is expressed in verses 33–34: *33So you shall not pollute the land where you are; for blood defiles the land, and no atonement can be made for the land, for the blood that is shed on it, except by the blood of him who shed it. 34Therefore do not defile the land which you inhabit, in the midst of which I dwell; for I the LORD dwell among the children of Israel.*

Deuteronomy 21:18–22

18"If a man has a stubborn and rebellious son who will not obey the voice of his father or the voice of his mother, and who, when they have chastened him, will not heed them: 19Then his father and his mother shall take hold of him and bring him out to the elders of his city, to the gate of his city; 20And they shall say to the elders of his city, 'This son of ours is stubborn and rebellious; he will not obey our voice; he is a glutton and a drunkard' 21Then all the men of his city shall stone him to death with stones, so you shall put away the evil person from among you, and all Israel shall hear and fear." Though this statement under the Law does not portray God's directions under grace, it does give us a view of God's concern for the holiness of His people; in addition, it reveals His attitude toward rebellion and toward parental responsibility.

Romans 13:4

Speaking of a ruler's role: *4For he is God's minister to you for good. But if you do evil, be afraid; for he does not bear the sword in vain; for he is God's minister, an avenger to execute wrath on him who practices evil.*

4. Death may come about purely by the breakdown of the human body, whether by war, violence, accident, suicide or illness.

Many examples of each of the above immediate causes of death are described in Scripture. Only one of each is included here.

War

1 Kings 22:34–37

Ahab, king of Israel, died in battle from a wound and the loss of blood.

Violence

2 Samuel 18:9–15

Absalom rode under the thick boughs of an oak tree which caught his hair and held him prisoner. Ten of Joab's armourbearers surrounded Absalom and killed him.

Accident

Luke 13:4

Jesus here refers to an accident well known to His hearers, in which eighteen were killed when the tower in Siloam fell. He further asks: *4... Think that they were worse sinners than all other men who dwelt in Jerusalem?* The implication is that their death was not because of sin.

Suicide

Matthew 27:5

[Judas] *cast down the pieces of silver in the temple, and departed, and went and hanged himself.*

Illness

2 Chronicles 16:12–13

[12]And Asa [king of Judah] *in the thirty and ninth year of his reign was diseased in his feet, until his disease was exceeding great: yet in his disease he sought not to the LORD, but to the physicians. [13]And Asa slept with his fathers, and died in the one and fortieth year of his reign* [a two–year illness.]

IV. THE DISPOSITION OF THE BODY

1. Burial is the most common Scriptural method for the disposition of the body.

a. Burial is mentioned many times in the Bible, in both Old and New Testaments.

Genesis 23:2–20

When Sarah died, Abraham was concerned to make proper arrangements for a suitable burial place for her. Though the sons of Heth would have given the land, Abraham insisted on paying what it was worth.

Genesis 25:8–10

When Abraham died, his sons Isaac and Ishmael, though they had not been close to one another, buried him in the same cave of Machpelah which Abraham had bought when Sarah died.

Genesis 35:19

Rachel, Jacob's wife who died on the trip back from Haran, was buried near Bethlehem, and memorialized by a pillar at her grave.

Genesis 35:29

After Jacob's return to his father Isaac, Jacob and Esau joined in burying him after his death.

Genesis 49:29–32, 50:2–14

Though Jacob died after he and his sons had moved to Egypt to be with Joseph, Jacob was very specific in instructing that he be buried in the cave of Machpelah, where also were buried Abraham, Sarah, Isaac, Rebekah, Leah. Joseph's compliance with his father's request is recorded in 50:2–14 and Acts 7:15.

Genesis 50:25–26

Though Joseph had become the prime minister of Egypt, he took an oath from the younger generation that when God finally delivered Israel from Egypt, they would take his bones back to Israel for burial. Their fulfillment of his wishes is recorded in Exodus 13:19 and Joshua 24:32, and referred to in Hebrews 11:22.

Deuteronomy 34:5–8

God buried Moses in the land of Moab, in a valley, and *[6]...no one knows his grave to this day.* Israel mourned for Moses for thirty days.

2 Samuel 3:31–39

When Joab murdered Abner, David commanded a mourning period in which he himself was very much involved. *[32]So they buried Abner in Hebron; and the king lifted up his voice and wept at the grave of Abner, and all the people wept.*

2 Samuel 21:12–14, 1 Samuel 31

The bodies of Saul and his three sons were found by the Philistines, with whom Israel was at war. The Philistines, in their rejoicing had fastened Saul's headless, naked body and those of his sons to a wall. Valiant men from Jabesh–gilead traveled all night to retrieve the bodies, burn them, and bury the bones (31:12–13). About 35 years later, David as king (21:12–14) *went and took the bones of Saul and the bones of Jonathan his son from the men of Jabesh–gilead... [13]And he brought up the bones...of those who had been hanged. [14]They buried the bones of Saul and Jonathan his son in the country of Benjamin in Zelah, in the tomb of Kish....*

1 Kings 2:10

David was buried in the city of David; i.e., in Bethlehem.

2 Chronicles 21:20

Jehoram, too, was buried in Bethlehem, but a distinction was made. He was not buried in a royal sepulchre because of his evil acts as king.

Matthew 8:21–22; Luke 9:59–60

In these passages, a disciple asked for permission to go first and bury his father before following the Lord. His meaning was to wait for his father to die, but the indication is also that the common method of disposing of the body was burial. So also in John 19:40.

Matthew 14:12

After John the Baptist was beheaded on order of Herod, *12Then his disciples came and took away the body and buried it.*

Matthew 26:12

When the woman anointed Jesus with precious ointment his disciples reprimanded her for such waste of valuable materials. It is evident that Jesus was expecting burial after His death, since he said, *12For in pouring this fragrant oil on My body, she did it for My burial.*

Matthew 27:59–60; Mark 15:46; Luke 23:53; John 19:38–42.

In each Gospel account, some details of Jesus' burial and the preparation for it are given. See also 1 Corinthians 15:4.

Acts 8:2

After Stephen's martyrdom, *2And devout men carried Stephen to his burial, and made great lamentation over him.*

Romans 6:4; Colossians 2:12

In each of these verses which explain the significance of baptism as representing our identification with Christ in His death and resurrection, the expression *buried with him by* [or in] *baptism* is used, showing the close connection between death and burial.

b. Not to be buried is represented as a disgrace.

2 Kings 9:10

In Elisha's prophecy of judgment on the house of Ahab, and on Jezebel his wife, he said, *10The dogs shall eat Jezebel...and there shall be none to bury her.*

Psalm 79:2

A description of the insults imposed upon the people of Jerusalem by other nations: *2The dead bodies of Your servants They have given as food for the birds of the heavens, The flesh of Your saints to the beasts of the earth.*

Proverbs 30:17

God's judgment upon one who despises his parents is said to be the exposure of his body to the birds, rather than burial.

Ecclesiastes 6:3

If a man begets a hundred children and lives many years, so that the days of his years are many, but his soul is not satisfied with goodness, or indeed he has no burial, I say that a stillborn child is better than he.

In various of the prophecies by Isaiah, Jeremiah and Ezekiel, one of the aspects of God's judgment was to be the lack of burial of dead bodies, with the resulting pollution of the land and the preying of flesh eating birds and animals. For examples, see the following: Isa. 14:19; Jer. 7:33, 16:4, 22:19, 25:33, 34:20; Ezek. 39:11–16.

c. Burials were often attended by friends and relatives.

Many of the previously noted passages illustrate this fact. In addition, see 1 Kings 14:13, where all Israel mourned for the son of Jeroboam; see also Luke 7:12–13, mourning for the son of the widow of Nain.

d. Many types of burying places are mentioned.

In the passages noted previously, and in additional ones which you can find by consulting *Nave's Topical Bible,* or a Bible encyclopedia, note the following: burial on hills, in valleys, in gardens, in houses, under trees, in tombs or sepulchres, in caves, with older family members and alone.

2. **Cremation, wherever used in Scripture, is associated with those who have sinned flagrantly, or who have in some way disgraced God's people.**

Joshua 7:15, 25

When Achan was identified as the one who had sinned and thus caused Israel defeat at the hands of enemies at God's command (v. 15) *25...So all Israel stoned him with stones; and they burned them with fire after they had stoned them with stones.*

1 Samuel 31:12

The bodies of Saul and his sons, mutilated by the Philistines, were burned and then buried.

2 Kings 23:20

Josiah, as part of his reformation, killed the priests of the high places and burned their bodies.

Amos 2:1

God pronounced condemnation on Moab because they had burned the bones of the king of Edom into lime.

---

3. The use of spices, incense, and special garments or wrappings was often included in the preparation for burial.

---

2 Chronicles 16:14

When Asa died after a 41-year reign in Judah, *[14]They buried him in his own tomb, which he had made for himself in the City of David; and they laid him in the bed which was filled with spices and various ingredients prepared in a mixture of ointments. They made a very great burning for him.*

2 Chronicles 21:19

Jehoram was king of Judah after his father Jehoshaphat. Jehoram rather than following his godly father, followed the kings of Israel (v. 6) and was a wicked king. He had an incurable disease from which he suffered for two years before his death. *[19]...And his people made no burning for him, like the burning of his fathers.* In other words, the custom was the use of incense.

Jeremiah 34:5

Jeremiah promised King Zedekiah that his death would not be by the sword, that he would see the king of Babylon, and go to Babylon, and that as there were *the ceremonies of your fathers, the former kings who were before you, so they shall burn incense for you and lament for you....*

John 11:44

When Lazarus was raised, *he came out bound hand and foot with graveclothes, and his face was wrapped with a cloth. Jesus said to them, "Loose him, and let him go."*

Matthew 27:59; Mark 15:46; Luke 25:53; John 19:40

Each of these verses speaks of the work of Nicodemus and Joseph of Arimathea. They speak of buying linen, of using fine linen clothes, of wrapping the body, or winding in clothes, *as the custom of the Jews is to bury.*

Luke 24:12; John 20:5–7

After the resurrection, *Peter arose and ran to the tomb; and stooping down, he saw the linen cloths lying by themselves; and he departed, marveling to himself at what had happened.* John's account notes that the handkerchief that had been around His head, not lying with the linen cloths, but folded together in a place by itself.

Mark 16:1; Luke 23:55–56, 24:1; John 19:39–40

Spices were used by Nicodemus and Joseph of Arimathaea when they prepared the body of the Lord for burial; they were also brought by the women for anointing the body on the third day.

V. LIFE AFTER DEATH

---

1. The immaterial part of man, the soul and spirit, continues to live after the body dies.

Soul: That part of man with which he is conscious of things and people around him, including intellect, emotions and will.

Spirit: That part of man with which he responds to God.

a. Physical death is not the end; life continues.

2 Samuel 12:23

David, after the death of his child by Bathsheba, said, *[23]...I shall go to him, but he shall not return to me.*

Psalm 49:15

The Psalmist proclaims: *[15]But God will redeem my soul from the power of the grave: for He shall receive me.*

Psalm 73:24–25

[24]You will guide me with Your counsel, And afterward receive me to glory. [25]Whom have I in heaven but You? And there is none upon earth that I desire besides You.

Luke 9:30–31

Moses and Elijah appeared on the mount of transfiguration and talked with Jesus. They must have been alive to do so.

Luke 20:37–38 with Exodus 3:6

Jesus speaking to the Sadducees, who denied the resurrection: *37"Now even Moses showed in the burning bush passage that the dead are raised, when he called the Lord 'the God of Abraham, the God of Isaac, and the God of Jacob.' 38For He is not the God of the dead but of the living, for all live to Him."* The fact that Moses so named the Lord indicates the fact that he knew they were alive, though not in physical bodies.

Luke 23:43

Jesus promised the thief who turned to Him on the cross: *43...Today you will be with me in paradise.* Plainly the two of them would be somewhere together.

Luke 16:19–31

The incident of the rich man and Lazarus: *22So it was that the beggar died, and was carried by the angels to Abraham's bosom. The rich man also died and was buried; 23And being in torments in Hades, he lifted up his eyes and saw Abraham afar off, and Lazarus in his bosom.* From the whole passage, it is evident that after death the men were conscious, could see, think, and talk. It is also clear that the rich man was in torment and was concerned about his brothers. They were very much alive.

John 3:36

He who believes in the Son has everlasting life; and he who does not believe the Son shall not see life, but the wrath of God abides on him. The everlasting wrath of God means nothing, if the unbeliever is not alive.

2 Corinthians 5:1, 4, 8, 10

1For we know that if our earthly house, this tent, [i.e. our bodies] *is destroyed, we have a building from God, a house not made with hands, eternal in the heavens.... 4For we who are in this tent groan, being burdened, not because we want to be unclothed, but further clothed, that mortality may be swallowed up by life.... 8We are confident, yes, well pleased rather to be absent from the body and to be present with the LORD.... 10For we must all appear*

before the judgment seat of Christ: that each one may receive the things done in the body, according to what he has done, whether good or bad.

2 Timothy 4:6

Paul expected a crown of righteousness after he died, and expected that death was coming soon.

b. The kind of life we live after death, both immediately and later, depends on our responses to God's provision in this life.

John 3:3, 6, 16, 18, 36

Jesus speaking to Nicodemus: *3Unless one is born again, he cannot see the kingdom of God.... 6That which is born of the flesh is flesh; and that which is born of the Spirit is spirit.... 16For God so loved the world, that He gave his only begotten Son, that whoever believes in Him should not perish, but have everlasting life.... 18He who believes in Him is not condemned; but he who does not believe is condemned already, because he has not believed in the name of the only begotten Son of God.... 36He who believes in the Son has everlasting life; and he who does not believe the Son shall not see life, but the wrath of God abides on him.*

John 5:24

Most assuredly, I say to you, he who hears My word and believes in Him who sent Me has everlasting life, and shall not come into judgment, but has passed from death into life.

John 8:24

Jesus speaking to the Jews in the temple: *Therefore I said to you that you will die in your sins; for if you do not believe that I am He* [i.e., the Messiah], *you will die in your sins.*

1 John 5:11–12

11And this is the testimony: that God has given us eternal life, and this life is in His Son. 12He who has the Son has life; he who does not have the Son of God does not have life.

Revelation 20:11–15

John describing a future event: *11Then I saw a great white throne and Him who sat on it.... 12And I saw the dead, small and great, standing before God, and books were opened. And another book was opened, which is the Book of Life. And the dead were judged according to their works, by the things which were written in the books....* *15And anyone not found written in the Book of Life was cast into the lake of fire.*

See also Luke 16:19–31, which describes the state of the unbeliever immediately following death, and such passages as Philippians 1:21–22, which describe the condition of believers immediately following death.

c. For the believer, the soul and spirit go immediately to be with Christ, an experience better than life on earth.

Luke 16:22

Lazarus, in contrast to the rich man, went immediately to a place called "Abraham's bosom," obviously a place of rest and comfort.

Luke 23:43

When the thief requested to be with Christ in His kingdom, thus expressing faith in Him, Christ said, *Assuredly, I say to you, today you will be with Me in Paradise.*

2 Corinthians 5:1–8

1For we know that if our earthly house of this tent, is destroyed, we have a building from God, a house not made with hands, eternal in the heavens. 2For in this we groan, earnestly desiring to be clothed upon with our habitation which is from heaven ... 6knowing that while we are at home in the body we are absent from the Lord: 8We are confident, yes, well pleased rather to be absent from the body and to be present with the Lord.

Philippians 1:21, 23

21For to me, to live is Christ, and to die is gain.... 23For I am hard pressed between the two, having a desire to depart and be with Christ, which is far better.

d. For the unbeliever, the soul and spirit go immediately to a place of imprisonment and torment, with full consciousness.

God very graciously does not give us much detail concerning the state of those unbelievers who have died and are waiting to be reunited with their bodies.

Luke 16:19–31

This incident, told by the Lord Himself, indicates that the rich man could see Abraham and Lazarus; he was separated from them and could not reach them; he was in torment and crying for relief; he could remember his past life and his brothers; he was concerned for their future.

1 Peter 3:18–20 (NASB)

18For Christ also died for sins...having been put to death in the flesh, but made alive in the spirit; 19in which also He went and made proclamation to the spirits now in prison, 20who once were disobedient, when the patience of God kept waiting in the days of Noah, during the construction of the ark.... [Apparently the spirits now in prison referred to here are unbelievers from Noah's day.]

See also Psalm 55:15, 23.

e. Children who die before they knowingly sin go to be with the Lord.

2 Samuel 12:23

David, when asked why he did not fast now that his son was dead, said, *23But now he is dead, why should I fast? Can I bring him back again? I shall go to him, but he shall not return to me.* David expected to be in heaven (Psa. 23:6).

Matthew 18:3–6, 10

Jesus speaking to the disciples: *3Assuredly, I say to you, unless you are converted and become as little children, you will by no means enter the kingdom of heaven. 4Therefore whoever humbles himself as this little child is the greatest in the kingdom of heaven.... 10In heaven their angels always see the face of My Father who is in heaven....* [Here the word *angels* may refer to their spirits, as is true in Acts 12:15.] *14Even so it is not the will of your Father who is in heaven that one of these little ones should perish.*

Mark 10:13–16; See also Matthew 19:14; Luke 18:15–17

When the disciples rebuked those who brought young children to Jesus for His blessing, His response was: *14...Let the little children come to Me, and do not forbid them; for of such is the kingdom of heaven. These children were young enough for Him to take them in His arms* (v. 16).

2. The material part of every man, the physical body, will be resurrected and joined to the soul and spirit at a future time not known to man.

Daniel 12:2

And man of those who sleep in the dust of the earth shall awake, some to everlasting life, some to shame and everlasting contempt.

John 5:28–29

²⁸The hour is coming, in the which all who are in the graves will hear His voice, ²⁹And come forth—those who have done good, to the resurrection of life, and those who have done evil, to the resurrection of condemnation.

Acts 24:15

Paul, in defending himself before Felix, called attention to the fact that what he believed was what was written in the law and the prophets: *¹⁵...That there will be a resurrection of the dead, both of the just and the unjust.*

1 Corinthians 15:21–25

²¹For since by man came death, by Man also came the resurrection of the dead. ²²For as in Adam all die even so in Christ all shall be made alive. ²³But each one in his own order: Christ the firstfruits, afterward those who are Christ's at His coming. ²⁴Then come the end...

a. Believers whose bodies have died will receive resurrection bodies when Christ comes to take all who have eternal life to be with Him—at the Rapture of the Church.

1 Thessalonians 4:13–18

¹³But I do not want you to be ignorant, brethren, concerning those who have fallen asleep [have died], lest you sorrow as others who have no hope. ¹⁴For if we believe that Jesus died and rose again, even so God will bring with Him those who sleep [are dead] in Jesus. ¹⁵For this we say to you by the word of the Lord, that we who are alive and remain until the coming of the Lord will by no means precede those who are asleep. ¹⁶For the Lord Himself shall descend from heaven with a shout, with the voice of the archangel, and with the trumpet of God. And the dead in Christ will rise first: ¹⁷Then we who are alive and remain shall be caught up together with them in the clouds, to meet the Lord in the air. And thus we shall always be with the Lord.

1 Corinthians 15:51–54

⁵¹We shall not all sleep [die], but we shall all be changed, ⁵²In a moment, in the twinkling of an eye, at the last trump. For the trumpet will sound, and the dead will be raised incorruptible, and we shall be changed.... ⁵⁴So when this corruptible has put on incorruption, and this mortal has put on immortality, then shall be brought to pass the saying that is written: "Death is swallowed up in victory."

Other passages that speak specifically of the resurrection of the bodies of believers include Luke 20:34–38; John 6:39–40, 44, 54; Romans 8:11; 2 Corinthians 5:10.

b. Believers who have trusted Christ during the Great Tribulation, after the Rapture, and who have been martyred for their faith, will be raised at the end of the Tribulation and before the millennial reign begins.

Revelation 20:4–6

⁴And I saw thrones, and they sat on them, and judgment was committed to them. And I saw the souls of those who had been beheaded for their witness to Jesus and for the word of God, who had not worshiped the beast or his image, and had not received his mark on their foreheads or on their hands. And they lived and reigned with Christ for a thousand years. ⁵...This is the first resurrection. ⁶Blessed and holy is he who has part in the first resurrection. Over such the second death has no power, but they shall be priests of God and of Christ, and shall reign with Him a thousand years.

c. The resurrection bodies of believers will be recognizable, made of flesh and bones, yet changed and freed from limitations common to men today.

Recognizable

Job 19:25–27

Job expected to recognize his Redeemer after his body had disintegrated. See also 2 Samuel 12:23.

Mark 16:9, 12, 14; Luke 24:31, 36–45

Jesus in His resurrection body was recognized by Mary Magdalene, two on the way to Emmaus, and the eleven.

John 20:11–18, 20, 26–29; 21:7, 14

John records the fact that He was recognized by Mary Magdalene, disciples in the upper room, Thomas, and several disciples who were fishing.

See also Acts 7:55–56.

Note that in several cases they did not quickly recognize Him; there were evidently changes that had taken place; yet they did know Him.

Made of flesh and bones

Matthew 28:9

The disciples held him by the feet and worshiped him.

Luke 24:30–31, 39, 41–43

Jesus, in His resurrected body, sat at the table, blessed the food, broke it and distributed to them; the disciples were invited to handle his body; He said He had flesh and bones, as no mere spirit has; He asked for food, and ate fish and honey in their presence.

John 20:20, 27; 21:9, 13

He showed the disciples his Hands and side and they recognized the wounds; He invited Thomas to handle His hands and side; He built a fire and distributed fish and bread to the disciples on the shore.

1 John 3:2

Beloved, now we are children of God; and it has not yet been revealed what we shall be, but we know that when He is revealed, we shall be like Him, for we shall see Him as He is.

Changed; freed from limitations

Matthew 22:30 and Luke 20:34–35

No marriage: *30For in the resurrection they neither marry, nor are given in marriage, but are like the angels of heaven.*

Luke 20:36

No death: *36Nor can they die anymore, for they are equal to the angels and are sons of God, being sons of the resurrection.*

Luke 24:13–31

No recognition when desired: Here, two disciples who had known the Lord before His death walked along with Him, talked with Him, discussed the Old Testament prophecies, sat down to eat together, and yet did not recognize Him until He so desired. See also John 21:4, 12.

Luke 24:31, 36; John 20:19, 26

No barriers: Jesus was able to vanish suddenly from the room in Emmaus; He appeared to groups suddenly, even when the doors were shut.

Romans 8:18, 23; 2 Corinthians 5:1–5

No suffering: Now redeemed, with no more groaning because of the sufferings of this life, and the desire for a body that does not limit us.

1 Corinthians 15:35–45

Related to our old bodies. Related in the same way that a seed that is planted is related to the new plant. Each one different; incorruptible or not subject to deterioration, powerful rather than weak, glorified, controlled by the spirit.

Philippians 3:20–21

20We also eagerly wait for the Savior, the Lord Jesus Christ: 21Who will transform our lowly [or, humiliating] body, that it may be conformed to His glorious body, according to the working by which He is able even to subdue all things to Himself.

Revelation 21:4

And God will wipe away every tear from their eyes; there shall be no more death, nor sorrow, nor crying; and there shall be no more pain, for the former things have passed away.

d. The bodies of unbelievers will be raised 1000 years after the Tribulation saints, at the end of the thousand-year reign of Christ on earth.

Revelation 20:4-6

In verse 4, those saved during the Tribulation are described as joining in the reign with Christ for a thousand years. *5But the rest of the dead did not live again until the thousand years were finished.* These are obviously the unbelieving dead, who did not rise before and who do not participate in the millennial reign with Christ.

e. Unbelievers, after their resurrection, will appear at the Great White Throne, be judged according to their works, and then cast into the lake of fire forever.

All will be included

Revelation 20:12–13. The dead, small and great, those buried in the sea, those already dead and in Hades—all stand before God.

Works will be considered in the judging (i.e., there will be degrees of punishment.)

Revelation 20:12–13 ...*and books were opened...And the dead were judged according to their works, by the things which were written in the books.*

Luke 12:47–48

The principle of judgment according to degree of disobedience.

All will be cast into the lake of fire

Revelation 20:15

And anyone not found written in the Book of Life was cast into the lake of fire.

Revelation 21:8

After a description of the blessings of those who will be included in the new heavens and new earth, and one more invitation for people who are athirst to come to the Savior, comes this pronouncement: *[8]But the cowardly, unbelieving, abominable, murderers, sexually immoral, sorcerers, idolaters, and all liars shall have their part in the lake which burns with fire and brimstone, which is the second death.*

VI. POST-RESURRECTION EVENTS FOR BELIEVERS

For a study of coming events, consult a standard theology book, or a book summarizing Bible doctrine. Look in the section on "last things," or "eschatology." One particularly helpful book is *Jesus Is Coming*, by W. E. Blackstone (Revell).

The following summary may be helpful:

1. Believers, in their new bodies, along with those living at the time and now changed, will be caught up together in the clouds, to meet the Lord in the air, and then be forever with Him in bodily form.

1 Corinthians 15:52; 1 Thessalonians 4:13-18; John 14:3

2. Believers will join in celebration of the culmination of their union with Christ, in the Marriage Supper of the Lamb.

Revelation 19:7–9

Here, the event is described; in other passages the concept of believers as the bride of Christ is presented: Matt. 22:2–14, 25:10; 2 Cor. 11:2; Eph. 5:25–32.

3. Believers will appear before the judgment seat of Christ to be judged for their lives and service and for the presentation of rewards.

2 Corinthians 5:10

For we must all appear before the judgment seat of Christ; that each one may receive the things done in the body, according to what he has done, whether good or bad.

See also Daniel 12:3; Matt. 12:36; Rom. 14:10–12; 1 Cor. 3:12–15; Gal. 6:7–8; Col. 3:24–25. The judgment here is for rewards, or loss of reward, not for salvation.

4. Believers will be identified with Christ as He reveals Himself to the world and establishes His millennial kingdom on earth.

Colossians 3:4

When Christ, who is our life, appears, then you also will appear with Him in glory.

Revelation 19:11–16

[11]Then I saw heaven opened, and behold, a white horse. And He who sat on him was called Faithful and True ... [13]and his name is called The Word of God. [14]And the armies in heaven, clothed in fine linen, white and clean, followed Him on white horses.

See also Zechariah 14:4–7; 1 Thessalonians 3:13; 2 Timothy 2:12; Jude 14; Revelation 17:14.

5. Believers will participate in the new heaven and new earth, free from limitations due to sin, in a special place prepared by the Lord for His own.

Revelation 21:1–27, 22:1–7

These chapters describe the place and the conditions in the new abodes, including the Holy City coming down from God out of heaven.

John 14:2, 17:24; Romans 8:18; Hebrews 11:10, 16; 13:14 are among the many passages which refer to the eternal state of believers of all ages.

VII. GOD'S POWER OVER DEATH

1. God's authority over death has been demonstrated on many occasions both independently and through His servants.

a. The Bible records many instances of God's use of death as judgment for sin.

Specific references are included in an earlier section of this chapter, under the heading "Causes of Death."

b. The Bible records many occasions when, through the power of God, someone was raised from the dead.

Examples:

1 Kings 17:17–24

Elijah prayed for the widow's son, asking, *21"O LORD my God, I pray, let this child's soul come back to him." 22Then the LORD heard the voice of Elijah, and the soul of the child came back to him, and he revived.... 24Then the woman said to Elijah, "Now by this I know that you are a man of God, and that the word of the LORD in your mouth is truth."*

2 Kings 4:32–37

Elisha prayed to God and He restored the son of the Shunamite woman to life.

Matthew 9:18–26; Mark 5:35–43; Luke 8:41–56

Jesus raised the daughter of Jairus, when already the professional mourners had gathered.

Luke 7:11–15

Jesus raised the son of the widow of Nain on the way to his burial.

John 11:1–37

Jesus raised Lazarus after he had been dead four days.

Acts 9:36–42

Peter was used by the Lord in the raising of Dorcas with the result that many believed in the Lord (v. 42).

2. God's power over death, as demonstrated in the resurrection of Christ, is presented as the basis for our faith.

Basis for our faith: 1 Corinthians 15:14–19
Basis for new life in Christ: 1 Corinthians 15:21–22; 2 Timothy 1:10
Basis for our resurrection: 1 Corinthians 15:12–13, 22–27; 2 Timothy 1:10
Basis for the defeat of Satan: Hebrews 2:14–15
Basis for victory in our lives: 1 Corinthians 15:57–58; Ephesians 1:19–21
Here is the measure of the power available to believers.

VIII. THE BELIEVER'S ATTITUDE TOWARD PHYSICAL LIFE AND DEATH

1. Life is short; we must use it wisely.

Job 20:4–7

For the wicked: *4Do you not know this of old... 5That the triumphing of the wicked is short, and the joy of the hypocrite is but for a moment? 6Though his haughtiness mounts up to the heavens, and his head reaches to the clouds; 7Yet he will perish forever like his own refuse: those who have seen him will say, 'Where is he?' "* (See also 21:13, 23; 24:24; 34:20.)

Psalm 37:2, 10, 35–36

2For they [evildoers] *shall soon be cut down like the grass, and wither as the green herb.... 10For* *yet a little while, and the wicked shall be no more; Indeed, you will look diligently for his place, But it shall be no more.... ³⁵I have seen the wicked in great power, and spreading himself like a native green tree. ³⁶Yet he passed away, and, behold, he was no more, Indeed I sought him, but he could not be found.*

Psalm 39:4

LORD, *make me to know my end, and what measure of my days, That I may know how frail I am.*

Psalm 89:47

Remember how short my time is: For what futility have You created all the children of men?

Psalm 90:10, 12

¹⁰*The days of our lives are seventy years; And if by reason of strength they are eighty years, Yet their boast is only labor and sorrow; For it is soon cut off, and we fly away.... ¹²So teach us to number our days, that we may gain a heart of wisdom.*

Proverbs 27:1

Do not boast about tomorrow, for you do not know what a day may bring forth.

John 9:4

Jesus speaking: *I must work the works of Him who sent Me while it is day; the night is coming when no one can work.*

James 1:10–11

¹⁰*[Let the rich rejoice] in his humiliation, because as a flower of the field he will pass away. ¹¹For no sooner has the sun risen with a burning heat than it withers the grass; its flower falls, and its beautiful appearance perishes. So the rich man also will fade away in his pursuits.*

James 4:13–15

¹³*Come now, you who say, "Today or tomorrow we will go to such and such a city, spend a year there, buy and sell, and make a profit"; ¹⁴Whereas you do not know what will happen tomorrow. For what is your life? It is even a vapor that appears for a little time and then vanishes away.*

1 Peter 1:24

All flesh is as grass, and all the glory of man as the flower of the grass. The grass withers, and its flower falls away.

2. Life is dependent on God—for its enablement and for its length.

a. For its enablement

Job 34:14–15

¹⁴*If He [God] should set His heart on it, if He should gather to Himself His Spirit and His breath; ¹⁵All flesh would perish together, and man would return to dust.*

Psalm 104:29–30

²⁹*You hide Your face, they are troubled; You take away their breath, they die and return to their dust. ³⁰You send forth Your Spirit, they are created* [baptism is used, showing the close connection between death and burial.]

Isaiah 40:6–8

⁶*All flesh is grass, and all its loveliness is like the flower of the field: ⁷The grass withers, the flower fades, because the breath of the LORD blows upon it; surely the people are grass.* (See also 1 Peter 1:24.)

b. For its length

See earlier section, under "Causes of Death," dealing with God's use of death in judgment.

Numbers 20:23–29, 27:12–14; Deuteronomy 34:5–7

It was God who determined when and where Moses and Aaron should die; in Moses' case at least, there was no physical reason for his death at this time.

2 Kings 22:19–20

In the reign of Josiah the book of the Law was discovered and read. As a result, Josiah wanted to know if the judgments pronounced there would come to pass. God answered through a prophetess saying, ¹⁹*"Because your heart was tender, and you humbled yourself before the LORD...and you tore your clothes and wept before Me, I also have heard you,"* says the LORD, ²⁰*"Surely, therefore, I will gather you to your fathers,...and your eyes shall not see all the calamity which I will bring on this place."*

Job 14:5

His days are determined, the number of his months is with You; You have appointed his limits, so that he cannot pass.

Isaiah 38:1

When Hezekiah was sick, the Lord sent Isaiah to him saying, *¹"Thus says the LORD: 'Set your house in order, for you shall die and not live.' "*

Philippians 2:27

Paul speaking of Epaphroditus: *²⁷For indeed he was sick almost unto death; but God had mercy on him, and not only on him but on me also, lest I should have sorrow upon sorrow.*

3. The closing of life sometimes brings insights of special significance.

Genesis 27:1–4, 26–29, 39–40

Isaac blessed Jacob and Esau, telling each one something of his future. In this case death did not come soon, as Jacob spent at least fourteen years in Haran and then returned to Isaac (35:27).

Genesis 49:1–33

Jacob, on his deathbed blessed each of his twelve sons, including some insight as to his future. (See also Hebrews 11:21.)

Genesis 50:24–25

Joseph reminded his sons of the fact that God would bring them out of Egypt, and took an oath of them that they would carry his bones back to Israel.

Deuteronomy 31:14–30, 32:1–52, 33:1–29, 34:1–7

In these chapters, God through Moses gave instruction and warning to all Israel, and to the Levites and priests, and to Joshua, his successor in leading Israel. He also included a song which God had commanded him to write as a way of teaching succeeding generations and warning them against apostasy (31:19–20).

1 Kings 2:1–9

David, before his death, charged Solomon with the responsibility of obeying the Lord; he also urged him to take vengeance on Joab and show kindness to Barzillai, who had helped him.

Acts 7:55–60

Stephen, when he was being stoned, saw the glory of God, and Jesus standing on the right hand of God, *⁵⁶And said, "Look! I see the heavens opened and the Son of Man standing at the right hand of God...."* *⁵⁹And they stoned Stephen as he was calling on God and saying, "Lord Jesus, receive my spirit. ⁶⁰...Lord, do not charge them with this sin."*

2 Timothy 4:6–8

Paul gave testimony to his own faithfulness and his expectation of a crown of righteousness, which the Lord, the righteous Judge, will give to *me on that Day, and not to me only but also to all who have loved His appearing.*

4. Death is not to be feared by believers, though it is rightfully feared by those who are not trusting the Savior.

a. No fear for believers

Psalm 16:11

You will show me the path of life; In Your presence is fullness of joy, At Your right hand are pleasures forevermore.

Psalm 23:4

Yea, though I walk through the valley of the shadow of death, I will fear no evil; For You are with me; Your rod and Your staff, they comfort me.

Psalm 31:5

Into Your hand I commit my spirit; You have redeemed me, O LORD God of truth.

1 Corinthians 15:55–57

⁵⁵O death, where is your sting? O Hades, where is your victory? ⁵⁶The sting of death is sin; and the strength of sin is the law. ⁵⁷But thanks be to God, who gives us the victory through our Lord Jesus Christ.

2 Corinthians 5:8

...Well pleased rather to be absent from the body and to be present with the Lord.

Philippians 1:21, 23

Paul's testimony as he approached death: *²¹For to me to live is Christ, and to die is gain.... ²³For I am hard pressed between the two, having a desire to depart and be with Christ, which is far better.*

Hebrews 11:13

All of God's promises are not fulfilled in this life, as witness many of the faithful listed in Hebrews 11.

Revelation 14:13

The Apostle John was commanded to write: *Blessed are the dead who die in the Lord from now on: ...they may rest from their labors, and their works follow them.*

See also Isaiah 57:1–2; 2 Timothy 4:8; Hebrews 2:15.

b. Rightful fear for unbelievers

Hebrews 9:27

...It is appointed for men to die once, but after this the judgment.

See also V, Concept ld and Concept 2e.

5. The death of His saints is precious to the Lord.

Psalm 116:15

Precious in the sight of the LORD is the death of His saints.

Philippians 1:20

Paul's hope was that above all else, Christ should be magnified in his body, whether by life or by death.

6. Doing God's will day by day is more important than whether we live or die.

Romans 14:8

For if we live, we live to the Lord; and if we die, we die to the Lord. Therefore, whether we live or die, we are the Lord's.

Philippians 1:21–26

²¹For to me, to live is Christ, and to die is gain. ²²But if I live on in the flesh, this will mean fruit from my labor; yet what I shall choose I cannot tell. ²³For I am hard pressed between the two, having a desire to depart and be with Christ, which is far better: ²⁴Nevertheless to remain in the flesh is more needful for you....

Hebrews 11:13–14, 39–40

After a list of some in the "hall of fame": *¹³These all died in faith, not having received the promises, but having seen them afar off, were assured of them, embraced them, and confessed that they were strangers and pilgrims on the earth. ¹⁴For those who say such things declare plainly that they seek a homeland.*

Then after a further list, many of whom were martyrs: *³⁹And all these, having obtained a good testimony through faith, did not receive the promise: ⁴⁰God having provided something better for us, that they should not be made perfect apart from us.*

PROJECT (for high school):

Obtain a copy of the Humanist Manifesto I and II, two statements of belief signed by persons who do not believe in a supernatural God. Study what they say about death, and what is implied by what they say. What Biblical truths about death and life after death are they refusing to believe? (Copies of these documents are available from the American Humanist Association, 7 Harwood Avenue, Amherst, N.Y. 14226, current price fifty cents for both.)

"Death will never take me by surprise. Christ has not led me so tenderly thus far, to forsake me at the very gate of Heaven."
—Adoniram Judson.